A SOFTER STRENGTH

A SOFTER STRENGTH

DONDI SCUMACI

CHARISMA
HOUSE

Most CHARISMA HOUSE BOOK GROUP products are available at special quantity discounts for bulk purchase for sales promotions, premiums, fund-raising, and educational needs. For details, write Charisma House Book Group, 600 Rinehart Road, Lake Mary, Florida 32746, or telephone (407) 333-0600.

A SOFTER STRENGTH by Dondi Scumaci
Published by Charisma House
Charisma Media/Charisma House Book Group
600 Rinehart Road
Lake Mary, Florida 32746
www.charismahouse.com

Unless otherwise noted, all Scripture quotations are from *The Message: The Bible in Contemporary English*, copyright © 1993, 1994, 1995, 1996, 2000, 2001, 2002. Used by permission of NavPress Publishing Group.

Scripture quotations marked KJV are from the King James Version of the Bible.

Scripture quotations marked NIV are from the Holy Bible, New International Version. Copyright © 1973, 1978, 1984, International Bible Society. Used by permission.

Scripture quotations marked NKJV are from the New King James Version of the Bible. Copyright © 1979, 1980, 1982 by Thomas Nelson, Inc., publishers. Used by permission.

Cover design by Justin Evans
Design Director: Bill Johnson

Visit the author's website at www.dondiscumaci.com.

Library of Congress Cataloging-in-Publication Data:
Scumaci, Dondi.
  A softer strength / Dondi Scumaci.
      p. cm.
  Includes bibliographical references (p.   ).
  ISBN 978-1-61638-491-3 (trade paper) -- ISBN 978-1-61638-575-0 (e-book) 1. Christian women--Religious life. I. Title.
  BV4527.S295 2011
  248.8'43--dc23

                                    2011024503

Portions of this book were previously published as *Designed for Success*, copyright © 2008, Excel Books, ISBN 978-1-59979-237-8.

11 12 13 14 15 — 9 8 7 6 5 4 3 2 1
Printed in the United States of America

Contents

What Glass Ceiling?

Let your light so shine before men, that
they may see your good works and
glorify your Father in heaven.

—MATTHEW 5:16, NKJV

GOD MADE YOU uniquely who you are on purpose and for a purpose. Psalm 139:15–16 says, "You know me inside and out, you know every bone in my body; you know exactly how I was made, bit by bit, how I was sculpted from nothing into something. Like an open book, you watched me grow from conception to birth; all the stages of my life were spread out before you, the days of my life all prepared before I'd even lived one day."

You were designed for success in all of your roles. Your work as a mother, mentor, professional, leader, or volunteer should be challenging and inspiring. You have unique strengths, and your opportunities are waiting! But maybe you aren't feeling that way about your life or your work. You work hard—you are the perfect picture of reliability and responsibility. Your friends, family, ministry partners, and coworkers count on you, and somehow you make it all happen. Most of the time you make it look easy.

Are you in love with what you are doing? Do you feel empowered and engaged? Are you making an impact—adding real value? Or are you feeling reactive? Do you find yourself monitoring rather than motivating? Begging (or settling) rather than negotiating? Feeling stifled and undervalued rather than impassioned and influential?

This does not have to be your story. You do not have to settle for less than what you were designed for. You are a powerful woman of God. Your gifts and talents have a purpose that is uniquely your own! As you begin to renew your thinking about what is available to you, you will find that you do not need to beg, become aggressive, or sit on the sidelines of your life. You have options! You can be fully engaged as the woman of God you are.

There is something very special about being a woman. There is strength in your femininity! You do not need to exchange that strength to gain opportunity, acceptance, or promotion.

It is my desire that, throughout these pages, you will

see you can be expressly who you are created to be *and* make a huge, measurable impact.

Whether you are a woman in ministry, a stay-at-home mom, a professional, or a blend of these, there is power and strength in you...just the way you are. There are also skills you can learn to create more confidence and increase your personal impact. These skills will also help you inspire and empower those around you.

Success is not a masculine right, and reaching your potential, your goals, being heard, and living your purpose are not things you have to forfeit or sideline because you're a woman. Some women have tried the "I'll-just-have-to-be-more-like-a-man" approach. They emulate the attitudes and behaviors of men—even successful men. This does not guarantee success. In fact, this strategy can backfire. When a woman does not act as expected, the impression is often very negative.

That explains it! When a man communicates aggressively, it is more acceptable than when a woman communicates aggressively. Compare your thoughts toward a driven, results-oriented male leader versus a driven, results-oriented woman. Who gets the fastest cooperation and the least amount of resistance?

In a way, we all contribute to this double standard. The truth is, we don't necessarily appreciate aggressive communication from anyone. It comes down to expectation. We accept what we expect.

The ultimate goal is not to be less feminine or more masculine. It is to be mindful of expectations, maximize your strengths, and develop the qualities that enhance your place as a powerful woman of God.

If we take a closer look at women in key leadership, ministry, or volunteer roles, we will see that these women are successful because they have held on to their feminine qualities while developing abilities that have been more traditionally attributed to men, such as confidence, assertiveness, and the ability to think strategically. These women know that their job is not to change what other people think or believe, but to invite people to see them differently—and keep inviting until they RSVP.

A LESSON FROM A QUEEN

Consider the story of Queen Esther in the Bible. This is a woman who could have reasonably excused herself from her challenge by claiming a "glass-ceiling exemption." She went from being an orphan girl to reigning as a queen! How did she break through the barriers? She lived in a time when stepping out of the traditional role could be fatal—literally!

There is much to learn from Queen Esther. When she learned of a plot to destroy the Jewish people, she was courageous and strategic. She had a sponsor, a very effective network, and a strong system of support. She prepared diligently and patiently implemented her plan.

Queen Esther was motivated by strong purpose, not self-promotion or self-preservation. Trace the steps of her path, and you will find months of preparation, a willingness to accept guidance, and the courage to take bold action. It is also interesting to note that, in that defining moment, with everything to gain or lose, people placed complete confidence in her ability to change the course of history.

I encourage you to study the lives and work of successful women. You may find them in history, in your neighborhood, or just down the hall from your office. How did they break through? What sets them apart? What characteristics and abilities are they known for?

One day someone could seek you out to learn how you changed the course of history in your world. You are a powerful, world-changing woman of God, and when you are performing at your personal best and feel at home in your skin, you are testifying to the glory of God that is active in your life and in the world.

A lot of my stories and examples are based on my experience as a corporate consultant. I have shared in the lives of incredible, multilayered women who are living life and learning from it. I pray you will glean from their stories the message God has specially crafted for you.

So come with me and let your light shine!

CHAPTER 1

Soften Your Inner Dialogue

*You'll do best by filling your minds and
meditating on things true, noble, reputable,
authentic, compelling, gracious—the best,
not the worst; the beautiful, not the ugly;
things to praise, not things to curse.*

—Philippians 4:8

IMAGINE THAT WHEN you were born, you were given a box. The box is empty to begin with, but almost immediately people begin to put messages into it. Some of the messages make you feel strong and safe and powerful; others teach you to doubt yourself and your abilities.

Over time the box is filled with messages. Some are duplicates. You've received them more than once and from more than one person. One message tells you it's important to be popular, one reminds you to always be very polite, while another tells you to wait to be recognized—because bragging is very bad. Your messages warn you against making mistakes, rocking the boat, or being *pushy*—because nobody likes a bossy girl.

Now imagine shaking the box! The messages get all mixed up. That makes it hard to separate the encouraging, empowering messages from the negative, limiting ones.

You grow up and carry your box of messages to work, ministry, or marriage. You bring it to every relationship, challenge, and possibility. As you begin to use them, you discover that, for much of your life, the messages have been managing you. Now you must learn to manage them. This is essential when you realize your messages are always playing. They inspire and filter your communications—from the inside out.

Communicating powerfully can be a real struggle for women. We are socialized to develop less confidence, to be less independent, and to undervalue our capabilities and intelligence.[1] Even so, women can be dynamic communicators. You can be a dynamic communicator! This is exciting, because everything you do to improve your ability to communicate impacts your relationships and your results.

Communication is the cornerstone of personal effectiveness, and it's an inside-out job. What begins as an internal dialogue—what we believe about ourselves, say to ourselves, and expect for ourselves—becomes how we present ourselves to others. This presentation is both spoken and unspoken. We are always communicating— with or without words, and our communications shape and reinforce our expectations.

How we present ourselves becomes what others believe about us. And what others believe about us and our abilities shapes their responses to us. Finally, the responses we receive from others come back around to reinforce the original belief.

TAKE THE LIMITS OFF!

We all have them—beliefs, even unconscious ones, that hold us back. This is a little like driving down the freeway, seventy miles an hour, with the emergency brake fully engaged. You may be getting somewhere, but you are most certainly tearing up the car. The instructions in the owner's manual should read: "Locate the beliefs that limit you to release your inner brake."

When I began speaking professionally, I learned the hard way how beliefs impact performance. One of my self-limiting beliefs was: "It's very important for people to like you—to approve of you." With practice, I could take this belief to a whole new level: "It's the most terrible thing in the whole wide world if people don't absolutely love you, and they might not."

This belief drove my performance. Above anything else I desperately needed *everyone* in *every* audience to like me. I could receive thundering applause and wonderful feedback, but if I had one mediocre evaluation or if I didn't "feel the love," I would instantly turn that into a weapon and torture myself all the way home.

This is ridiculous behavior—really ridiculous and really painful behavior.

The obsessive need to be liked became the primary focus of my performance. It was like a drug. I was an approval addict, and my performance suffered.

I continued to struggle with this behavior until I identified the belief driving it. Then I understood: "It's not about people liking you. In fact, it's not about you at all! This is about them. It is about making a real difference."

All things are created twice. We create them first mentally, then physically. —Stephen Covey

With an audible sigh of relief, I mentally crossed out the rule "It's important to be liked" and replaced it with "It's important to make a lasting difference." I was free then to focus on the audience and on making a positive impact. I enjoyed my work more, and my performance improved.

How do you locate your self-limiting beliefs? Begin with what you believe about your

I am often misunderstood.

4

accomplishments, strengths, and abilities. What are you really good at? What achievements are you most proud of? What skills have you mastered?

Start with what you believe about yourself, and then listen to what you say to yourself.

TALK NICELY TO YOURSELF

Do you talk to yourself? Of course you do. We all do. Have you listened to that conversation lately? I dare you to keep a log of your self-talk for one week. You may be shocked at how mean you are to you!

The first step in managing your self-talk is to become more aware of it. This conversation has been going on for so long in your head, it's like background noise—elevator music! You don't even notice it anymore. Turn up the reception, and really listen to what you are saying. What do you say to yourself when...

- You make a mistake?

- You look in the mirror—naked?

- You forget something important?

- You say the wrong thing?

Once you have isolated the negative messages, replace them with positive, empowering ones. Imagine for a moment that your self-talk is like programming a computer. You are either programming yourself for success or failure, and your thoughts are like commands. Software designers know that a bad command in the program cannot be ignored. Until a bad command is replaced, it wreaks havoc in the program.

Our words have such power—more than we may ever realize. It is true, "Death and life are in the power of the tongue" (Proverbs 18:21, NKJV).

Never say anything to yourself or to anyone else that you do not sincerely wish to be true.

When you catch yourself saying, "I am so stupid," stop! Delete that message and replace it immediately. Tell yourself instead, "I am bright and intelligent and a fast learner."

Managing your internal dialogue is so important because you cannot be a dynamic, confident communicator when you are tearing yourself apart from the inside out. It is also important because that isn't just a critic living inside you—it's a prophet. As Stephen Covey teaches in *The Seven Habits of Highly Effective People*, all things are created twice. We create them first mentally, then physically.[2]

WHAT YOU BELIEVE WILL COME TO LIFE

You will also find self-limiting beliefs by taking an inventory of your expectations. When you try something new, do you expect to succeed? When obstacles block your path, do you expect to prevail? When something wonderful happens, do you expect it to last?

Have you ever said, "This is too good to be true," or "This won't last"? What you are really saying is, "I can't believe this is happening for me because I really don't believe I deserve it. I am not worthy of this good thing."[3]

> Several years ago at a conference on the West Coast, I noticed a group of women sitting in the middle of a large audience. They were from two local hospitals. I learned the hospitals were merging—all of these women were in a very vulnerable place. Some of them would not have jobs when the two organizations folded together.
>
> One woman in particular caught my eye. She was so engaged—so full of energy. On a break she introduced herself and a colleague. She was almost breathless when she said, "I am excited and terrified! My job at the hospital may be eliminated. This situation is pushing me way out of my comfort zone. For the first time in years I am thinking about what I would love to do."
>
> Her optimism was compelling and contagious. Then her associate spoke: "Yeah, you work for a company for twenty-five years, and they kick you to the curb six months before you retire." You could almost hear the vacuum as the oxygen was sucked from the room.
>
> About five months later I received an e-mail

from the first woman. She was writing to tell me exciting news. She had received a significant promotion with the merged organization. She was absolutely thrilled with her new job. I was not surprised.

When I wrote to congratulate her, I couldn't resist asking about her colleague. She replied, "Oh. Unfortunately she was in the first round of layoffs." Again, I was not surprised.

What is more tragic than this woman losing her job was that she left the organization believing that something had been done to her.

Here you have two women in the same situation experiencing very different outcomes. What accounts for the difference?

That isn't just a critic living inside you—it's a prophet.

One of them made empowered, accountable choices. One of them behaved like a victim. Both of them had a prophet inside predicting the future. Both of the prophecies came true.

You will find the beliefs that are limiting you by noticing what you believe about yourself, what you say to yourself, and what you expect for yourself. You release the internal brake by reflecting on your abilities, firing the critic, and managing the prophet.

This is where your communication turns from inside out. Next we will look at what you say about yourself—how you present yourself to others.

LEARN TO TALK APPROPRIATELY ABOUT YOUR STRENGTHS

Women want to be liked. To that end we may use modesty and self-depreciation as a communication bridge—a connection. Women also tend to overestimate the credentials and experience of others while discounting their own.

> I watched this scenario play out with one of my dearest friends. She is dynamic and beautiful, hardworking and extremely talented. For more than twenty years she has run a successful day care, assisted her husband in ministry, and is a freelance writer for a popular parenting magazine. Recently an opportunity was presented to her. Her response is a prime example of how women underestimate themselves and overestimate others.
>
> My friend was asked to consider consulting for a large organization because of the creative, intuitive way she works with her children and teachers. While she does not have a formal degree in this field, she has an amazing

God-born talent, countless certifications and licenses, and decades of successful experience. As she investigated the opportunity, she began to question her qualifications. "I don't have the formal training for this. The people in this company have incredible résumés." I gently—OK, maybe not so gently—reminded her that her own résumé was nothing short of incredible.

My dear friend did what many of us do. We supersize the value of others, but when it comes to our own value, we think in terms of the kid's meal!

We have all been turned off by people who are walking, talking, look-at-me billboards. The noise of it does not compel—it repels.

At the opposite end of the spectrum is complete obscurity—a lack of clarity, distinctness, and definition. Perhaps the answer is found somewhere in the middle—a gentle balance of humility and confidence, understanding when and how to communicate a sincere, authentic message that allows us to walk into the opportunities God has for us.

Here are some better ways to appropriately talk about your successes when you are offered a God-opportunity:

1. Instead of talking about what you did, talk about the difference it made.

2. Instead of talking about what you can't do, talk about what you can do and what you are learning to do.

3. Talk about your goals and how you will measure your success.

4. If you are working for an organization, debrief results with your boss candidly and without apology. Listen to the difference between these two approaches: "I think the project went all right. There were some rough spots, but we made it through." Compare that report with this one: "We met our objectives, and we learned a great deal. I am most proud of the way we..."

5. Quantify your results whenever you can. Instead of saying, "I think we will save a lot of money," say, "I estimate a savings of more than $10,000." This would come in handy with your spouse too, when its time for that new couch.

6. When you fall short of your goals, ask a friend or colleague for feedback, and talk about what you have learned from the

experience and how you will apply those insights in the future.

7. Talk about your weaknesses differently. Instead of saying, "I need to be more analytical," say, "I want to strengthen my analytical skills. What projects or assignments would help me do that?"

8. Even your challenges are opportunities to demonstrate creativity and problem-solving skills. When you aren't getting the results you need, couple the issues with recommendations and solutions.

False humility only strengthens the negative internal dialogue you may be working to overcome. When you are able to speak truthfully and humbly about your gifts, talents, and accomplishments, you begin to reinforce your God-given destiny and purpose. Your positive thoughts about yourself and the positive way you present yourself to others will begin to invite those next-level opportunities.

PREPARE FOR OPEN DOORS

Opening night on Broadway happens after weeks of exhaustive practice and rehearsal, making even the most difficult performance look effortless and completely natural. You have openings too. They may happen at any time. Prepare for them with carefully managed personal messages.

The most effective personal messages are deliberate, well crafted, and rehearsed. They are not off-the-cuff, fly-by-the-seat-of-your-pants speeches breathlessly delivered in the elevator. These are thoughtful messages highlighting your accomplishments, results, experiences, and contributions. These messages are chapters in a larger story—the story of who you are, what you have learned, what you do well, and what you value.

To build your messages, write down your:

1. Ten most significant accomplishments and achievements—yes, you do have ten!

2. Strengths and abilities—what you do well

3. Experiences and, more importantly, what you learned from them

4. Goals and aspirations

5. Projects you are working on now and the difference they will make for the organization—how they will directly impact the mission, vision, and bottom line

6. Interests and hobbies

7. Commitments to social or community initiatives and why you chose to support these causes

When you polish and put these messages together, you will have a story that reflects the best of you and expresses your passion. When people ask what you do for a living, what's the focus of your ministry, what are you passionate about, or why you chose this job, this story replaces what you've been saying—which, if you will admit it, has typically been your title, the name of the organization you serve, or the tasks or chores you perform every day. This is not what you do or who you are!

You may be surprised how difficult this task is, and that reinforces the importance of working through it. If it's hard to think of these pieces, you most certainly aren't talking about them, and that means you are missing opportunities to invite people to know who you are. Begin preparing your personal messages by developing five important stories:

1. What do you do?

2. What are you working on now?

3. What accomplishments are you most proud of?

LOVE AND!!
happiness

4. What are you learning?

5. Where do you see yourself in the future?

Your story is a part of communication you can plan for—a piece you can maximize and manage. These are the answers that can, and should, be on the tip of your tongue. Take advantage of that, because some answers won't be.

DON'T TELL TOO MUCH

We know that women communicate to connect—to create understanding and build relationships. To that end, we may be more willing to talk about our fears, feelings, and challenges. We use self-disclosure to make our connections more meaningful. We pull off our "masks" and make ourselves vulnerable to others. This makes us authentic and real. Our self-disclosure invites others to pull off their masks and be authentic and real with us.

In the right moment, self-disclosure can be a powerful communication tool. In the wrong setting, it is self-sabotage! In some situations, the willingness to throw up your hands, ask the question, and admit, "I don't get it," is like a breath of fresh air. In the wrong situation, it may create a perception of weakness or a lack of awareness.

Women are socialized to be more comfortable

showing emotions, while men are taught to control emotions.[4] Studies have even shown that women are more comfortable asking questions in front of a group, while men are more likely to search for the answer privately.

Use self-disclosure wisely and purposefully. Consciously choose when and with whom you will make yourself vulnerable. Use questions strategically as well. Before asking a question in front of the group, there are some things you may want to consider.

- Is this question timely and relevant?

- Am I asking this question because I really need to know or because I really need to connect?

- Is this a question or self-presentation?

- Does this question move the conversation forward or take the group off task?

- Do I need the answer right now, or can I make a note of it?

- Does my question reflect a desire to understand or a lack of preparation or awareness?

When it comes to self-disclosure, you'll want to carefully consider how much personal information to share in certain settings. Remember, the stereotypes have been working for a long time. You don't want to unintentionally reinforce them with your communications.

SPEAK IN POSITIVE TERMS

Another way to strengthen your internal dialogue is to make your external message positive. In some circles this is called speaking faith, because while you may have some doubts in your heart, your positive speech can help turn a light on, on the inside of you. Have you ever just smiled when you were having a bad day? What does that do for your spirit? It kind of shifts things a bit.

Reframing your verbal messages does something similar, and it goes a long way in all your relationships from home to work and then to church and ministry. But let me assure you, this is not a call for a Pollyanna, everything-is-so-wonderful approach. That is unrealistic, inauthentic, and just plain annoying. Sometimes things aren't wonderful. Sometimes things are absolutely awful. Even then you can frame your messages positively by talking about:

- What you want instead of what you *don't* want

- What you can do rather than what you *can't* do

- What you are as opposed to what you *aren't*

Listen closely, and you will notice how often we talk about what we don't want! We do this to our children when we say, "Don't get dirty." "Don't be late." "Don't get wet." Instead, why don't we say, "Stay clean," "Be on time," or "Stay dry."

Pay attention to how often people talk about what they can't do. You will hear things like, "That's against the policy." "We can't do that." "That's not possible." How much more compelling to say, "Our practice *is*..." "Here's what I *can* do..." "Here's how I *can* help..." There may be one hundred fifty things you can't do in a given situation. Talk about the one thing you can do!

Finally, talk about what you *are*. I am stunned at how often people put a negative spin on a positive message. When someone asks you how you are, do you say, "I can't complain"? Or do you say, "I feel great"? When a friend thanks you, is your reply, "No problem"? Or do you say, "My pleasure"?

I've become a collector of signs and phrases. I am always looking for good examples of positive and negative communication frames. I'll pack them and take them with me if they will fit in my carry-on!

The one that delights me the most is often found in hotels. Have you seen this sign? "All of the items in your room have been carefully inventoried. Any missing items will be added to your bill."

That makes me want to take a towel.

Listen to the difference when you put the message in a positive frame. This sign was found in the pocket of a hotel bathrobe: "This bathrobe has been provided for your comfort and convenience during your stay. If you love it and would like to take it with you, please let us know. We will be happy to wrap it and include it on your final statement."

Isn't the difference amazing? One message dares you to steal; one invites you to buy. One makes you an enemy; the other makes you a customer.

I found another great example on the inside of a very dirty window in Manhattan. This was a dry cleaner, and the hand-scrawled sign said, "We close at 9:00 p.m." I wanted to quietly replace the sign with one that said, "We are *open* until 9:00 p.m." Unfortunately I could not. It was 9:05 p.m.

Think of it this way: the words you choose are like a compass. When you need your children to clean their room, your spouse to take the car in for service, or a donor to respond to a fund-raising request, how do you communicate that to them? The way you frame your words will send people in the direction you want them to go.

Turn your objections into questions.

If you have a coworker, friend, or ministry partner who is extremely opinionated and overbearing, you may be tempted to give in or push back. But again this is another opportunity to reinforce your internal dialogue with how you respond to others. Instead of objecting to their brash or opinionated ideas, there is another option—ask a question. Instead of saying, "This will cost too much," or "We've tried this before and it didn't work," say, "How will we pay for this?" or "How is this different from what we've tried in the past?"

You may experience something just short of a miracle with this strategy. You will find yourself working through even difficult issues more productively.

Another way to deal with very forceful people is to make force unnecessary. Use four of the most powerful words in the English language: "You may be right." Those words being said doesn't mean you think they are right. It just means you are willing to listen to what they have to say.

When you say those words, watch their weapons fall. You can almost see them relax. They were looking for a fight, and they didn't find one. Now you can turn your objections into questions, and another conflict may become collaboration.

Mentally rehearse success.

Especially when you are going into a difficult situation, mentally rehearse success. How do you want it to turn out? Picture yourself smiling and comfortably working through the issues. Imagine the others involved responding positively.

SEVEN WAYS TO SPEAK FROM A PLACE OF STRENGTH

1. Lose the verbal wince!

One sure sign of passive communication is what I call the verbal wince. This is when you apologize for what you are about to say. It sounds like this:

- "I'm not really sure, but I think…"

- "I could be wrong, but…"

- "This is just my opinion, but…"

You immediately strengthen your communication when you stop wincing!

2. Make eye contact.

This is not a stare down, just comfortable contact. When you fail to meet another's eyes, you look uncomfortable, insecure, or dishonest. Eye contact—or the lack of it—sends an important message.

3. Equalize the posture.

I learned this wonderful lesson from a nurse. She told me when people are sick and hurt in the hospital, they feel small and helpless. There they are lying in a bed or sitting in a wheelchair with people literally standing over them—talking *down at* them. She learned to equalize the posture by pulling up a chair and talking *to* her patients.

This is a simple way to become more assertive immediately. When someone is standing over you, rise to the occasion. When they are sitting, pull up a chair.

4. Memorize a confident posture.

What does confidence look like? Confidence stands straight, with shoulders squared, arms relaxed, and the chin up. Confidence does not rock back and forth—as if a baby were sitting on the hip. And it does not fidget with jewelry or locks of hair.

5. Be objective based in your communication.

Go into every communication with a clear objective. This is extremely valuable when the situation is emotionally charged. If you focus on the feelings, they may get the best of you. Focus instead on the objectives—on what you are trying to accomplish.

Another way to be objective based is to choose the right channel of communication. Communication channels are like the stations on your radio. We can communicate by e-mail, voice mail, or in person. Which channel is the best choice? It depends on your objective. If you want to inform or update, perhaps an e-mail or memo is the most efficient way. If you want to change hearts, minds, or behaviors, use the spoken word—preferably with eye contact attached.[5]

6. Eliminate nonwords and words you use too much.

Nonwords are filler words—words like *uh, um,* and *huh.* We use them to plug the holes of silence, and they weaken our message.

Most of us also have words or phrases we use too often. These are distracting. Listen for those and get rid of them.

7. Align your message for real impact.

Your mother was right. It's not just *what* you say but *how* you say it that matters too—it may matter more.

There have been many studies on the impact of words, tone, pace, and body language. Most of them generally agree on these important points:

- It's not just words that make a message.

- How you say it matters too.

- How you look while you say it matters more.

The visual message is most important for two reasons:

1. It gets there first and sets the stage for everything to follow.

2. If the words and the body don't match, the body will be believed.

That means when we ask how you are, and you say in a clipped, tight-lipped way, "Fine," we don't believe you.

Proper Alignment Between Your Internal and External Communication

Softening your inner dialogue is one of the most important parts of being an effective woman of God. It reflects how you see God and His ability to work through you and others to accomplish His purposes. It also influences how you present yourself to others and how you communicate with them.

You can prepare yourself for a great future full of opportunities, growth, and closer relationships by being consistent in what you know is true about you based on God's Word by thinking it first then acting it out in the way you relate to people.

CHAPTER 2

Empower and Equip Yourself

May [God] equip you with all you need
for doing his will. May he produce in you,
through the power of Jesus Christ, every
good thing that is pleasing to him.

—HEBREWS 13:21, NLT

WHEN YOU WERE growing up, did you have a kids' table set up for Thanksgiving dinner? You know, the side table designated for children at holiday dinners. The big table was reserved for grown-ups. And what a rite of passage it was to finally be invited to sit there!

Many women still feel like—or behave as if—they are sitting at the kids' table. We are waiting for an invitation to join the grown-ups.

It may be time for you to pull up your chair and ask for someone to pass the bread!

Right now you may be waiting for someone else to

empower you—to give you the things you need to be effective and to feel powerful. And right now I hope you will discover how to empower yourself and how you may be actually giving your power away.

Let's begin with a definition. *Empowerment* is defined as "equipping or supplying with ability; enabling."

We equip people with tools, information, skills, and confidence. We enable them through training, practice, feedback, support, and encouragement. Others empower us when they give us authority, independence, and even their trust. It's wonderful when that happens. But what if it doesn't?

Then you must look for ways to empower yourself and eliminate what is disempowering. Working from our definition of empowerment, that means you must go get the information, skills, and confidence you need; seek out opportunities to learn and practice; ask for feedback; and build a strong system of encouragement and support. There is much to be done!

> Shannon leads a customer service team for a large organization. This is a company that is head over heels in love with conference calls, and Shannon spends hours dialed in to these meetings every week. One of the calls she is required to attend is a complete waste of time. The information is either irrelevant or redundant.
>
> Shannon would like to stop attending the call, but she was told she should be there—or

it might look bad. So every Wednesday at one o'clock, she is present and accounted for.

I wish Shannon felt free to quit attending the meeting—without feeling guilty—or at the very least, free to offer feedback to make the meeting more productive. I am not suggesting that she defiantly announce she will not be attending these *ridiculous* meetings anymore. I am suggesting that she find a way to protect her time and productivity by professionally confronting anything that steals it.

Shannon is waiting to be excused from the table.

Katrina manages the volunteer ministry at a megachurch. Frequently she receives procedure and process updates. She is responsible for covering these changes with her group. After reviewing one of the latest change memos, she has real concerns. She discusses these with the other ministry leaders, and they don't see a problem. Reluctantly, she implements the changes with her team.

Almost immediately serious problems with the new procedure erupt. Everyone is thrown into damage-control mode, scrambling to fix the problems created by the change. Service is interrupted, and some of the church's needs are left undone.

When I asked Katrina why she didn't mention her concerns to the church administrator, she quietly said, "I didn't want him to think I was complaining about the changes, and besides, the other leaders thought it would be all right. I was the only one who thought there may be a problem."

Katrina trusted the judgment of others more than she trusted her own—she pushed the "snooze" button on her internal alarm. And she didn't want to appear negative by challenging authority. If she had found a way to do that, a crisis would have been avoided, time would have been saved, and the church members would have received the service they expect and deserve.

Katrina is waiting for permission and consensus.

Cindy supports several attorneys. Each of them is fast paced and results driven, and they rely heavily on her. Her work area is literally surrounded by the attorneys' offices. They rush by tossing assignments and instructions at her: "File this…call him…draft a letter to…" Cindy feels like she is working inside a pinball machine as she is bounced from one priority to another.

What is most disheartening is that none of the attorneys have a full appreciation for what she really does. Each of them only knows what she does for him or her, and all of them believe their work is the top priority. She stays late, comes in early, and frequently works weekends to catch up. Cindy makes it look easy, but it isn't.

Cindy is waiting for someone to realize her workload is out of hand and recognize what it takes to get it all done.

In each of these scenarios, you see hardworking, intelligent women giving their power away. Handing over power may look like:

- Waiting for someone to tell you it's OK to recommend a change

- Following the group, even when you sense the group should be going in a different direction

- Hoping someday, someone will notice how hard you are working

- Trusting others' judgment more than your own

EMPOWER YOURSELF WITH OPTIONS

We back ourselves into cramped corners when we think in terms of yes or no, this or that, do or don't. Always assume there are more options.

This is hard because we are taught to color in the lines. Keep it pretty and don't make a mess. In life and in business sometimes the best answer and the most productive response may be outside the lines.

I love the story about the man who wakes up in the middle of the night soaking wet. Realizing that his waterbed has sprung a leak, he gets up and, half asleep, wrestles the mattress down a flight of stairs and outside. Along the way, the mattress snags on something and rips beyond repair. To make matters worse, it is pouring down rain, and the man slips and falls in the mud. Now he is wet and muddy, sleep deprived, and "mattress-less."

The next day he purchases a new mattress and sets it up. Exhausted from a lack of sleep the night before, he falls gratefully into bed. In the middle of the night he wakes again—soaking wet. It's raining again. This is when he realizes there is a leak in the roof.

SOLVE THE RIGHT PROBLEM

Let's revisit the three scenarios above to identify the real problem and look for options "outside the lines."

Shannon's real problem isn't a conference call that wastes her time. Her real problem is that she doesn't feel powerful enough to do anything about it. *Appearances* have become more valuable than productivity. Shannon thinks she has two choices—attend the meeting or don't attend the meeting. What other options exist?

She could partner with coworkers who also attend the meeting. Perhaps they can rotate, each of them taking a turn and taking notes to update the others with a five-minute debriefing or an e-mail. She could provide feedback to make the meeting more valuable. She could ask for guidance. What should she be taking away from this meeting? How should she be using this information?

In Katrina's situation, the real problem isn't that she didn't speak up more and make a stronger stand. The real problem is *why*. When she looked at this situation, Katrina saw two clear options. One was to go with the flow and follow instructions. The other option was to be uncooperative and negative. Katrina wasn't unwilling to speak with the administrator about her concerns. But she didn't know how to do that without appearing to be negative. She also didn't want to challenge his authority, and she believed others knew more than she did.

What if Katrina went to the church administrator and established some communication ground rules? She might say, "I want to be someone you can count on to do the right things, to support the mission of the church, and to be solutions oriented. When we receive process changes and I have concerns with how those changes will impact us, what is the best way for me to communicate that?"

With this approach, Katrina is not asking permission to confront the issues. She is gaining agreement on how to confront issues effectively.

Katrina's case gives us another insight. Everyone—

including you—has a *unique* perspective. By that I mean, you will see things others may not see. And your perspective is a valuable resource to whomever you serve. Develop that perspective. Trust your judgment. Learn to present your concerns and ideas effectively.

In Cindy's case, the real problem isn't how many people she supports or the intense pace of the environment. Her problem is managing expectations and priorities. Cindy needs to make her daily plan more visible to her bosses. She could send a brief e-mail first thing in the morning highlighting the priorities of the day. When new tasks are thrown her way, she could ask for guidance. Pointing to her plan she might say, "I'll be happy to do this for you now. Will you help me reprioritize these tasks?" That is known as "upward delegation," and it is a marvelous way to manage multiple priorities with flexibility.

By the way, when men work on a Saturday, everyone knows. (This comes straight from the horse's mouth. Men do not want personal credit for this little tidbit, but the gents are my source.) They make a point to call their boss from the office. They don't tell the boss who else is there; they just make sure the boss knows they are there. They also send a periodic e-mail at 2:00 a.m. That doesn't mean they were working all night. They just want you to know they were thinking about work in the middle of the night.

EMPOWER YOURSELF BY
KNOWING YOUR ROLE

Because of my experience as a corporate consultant, I know the effects of not being sure of your role. When you don't know your role, you will not be able to be proactive, confident, or able to envision future success. You may be perceived as needing attention or reassurance, a poor problem-solver and decision-maker, lacking confidence, or trying to avoid responsibility. That is not attractive!

It is important to understand where you end and others begin, so that you can reach the desired outcome for a project at work, a mission in ministry, or a relationship at home. We seek validation and approval from others when we lack role clarity and we leave a piece of our credibility behind.

In my consulting practice, I use a very simple tool to empower people through role clarity. This is an informal discussion tool, and I like it because you can do it on a napkin at dinner. This exercise works. It's called the Roles Box. I modified it from its original form to account for the various roles you may want to clarify.

Whether you are the one in charge or a member of the team, you can use the Roles Box to empower yourself with clarity. Here's how it works.

Four quadrants are used to define and confirm

responsibilities. Begin by listing the things only other people can do and decide. If, for example, you are examining your role as team member, you would begin by thinking about the role of your leader. Next, list the things you can do and decide on your own—without permission or approval.

Roles Box	
These are the things only the key players (manager, pastor, spouse, board of directors, or ministry partner) can do or decide.	These are the things the team member can do and decide.
Recommends	**Informs**
These are things the leader will ultimately decide based on the team member's recommendations.	These are the things the team member can do while keeping the leader informed.

The Recommends box contains what the decision maker or lead person will ultimately decide, but team members can influence the decision with recommendations.

The Informs quadrant is for those responsibilities and decisions the team member can take care of independently while keeping the leader informed.

Once you complete the quadrants, you and your key

players should compare notes. You may find gaps in your expectations—that is a good thing. The Roles Box allows you to work through those differences and find clarity.

> In one experience with this exercise, a group of three supervisors and their boss—all were women—located significant gaps in perspective and expectation. These gaps were creating serious conflict. The manager was disappointed in what she believed was a lack of initiative and commitment on the part of her supervisory staff. The supervisors felt hesitant and unsupported. This was damaging their confidence in themselves and their leadership.
>
> After completing the Roles Box exercise, there was greater understanding, empowerment, and accountability. Everyone felt better.
>
> Because their roles were evolving, they continued to use the exercise periodically.
>
> As the supervisors gained experience and demonstrated sound judgment, they were given more latitude, authority, and independence. They found that what begins in the Recommends box may move to the Informs quadrant. What is handled exclusively by the manager may eventually shift to the Recommends quadrant, and so on.

I encourage you to try this exercise. Remember, as you grow and dreams and goals become realized, expectations will change. You will need to have this conversation more than once.

Initiating the Roles Box conversation prevents you from hesitating when you should take action and from stepping all over someone's feet with too much initiative. There is such thing as too much initiative.

What distinguishes positive initiative from the limiting kind? I think there are two things. One is motive; the other is wisdom.

It is entirely possible to rush in with the best of intentions and make a big mess. That happens when we don't see the bigger picture and consider the ripple effect of our actions. When we rush to act before thinking about the impact, that's a lack of wisdom and good judgment.

Initiative also backfires when motives are impure. If my actions are self-promoting or self-preserving, it won't look like initiative at all. It will look like political maneuvering or sabotage!

Check your motives, think it through, and demonstrate extreme initiative.

EMPOWER YOURSELF THROUGH PERSONAL ACCOUNTABILITY

In the parable of the talents, three servants are given responsibility. As their master is leaving on a journey, he entrusts each of them with his property—*according to their ability.* One of the servants is given five talents, one receives two talents, and a third is entrusted with a single talent.

It is interesting to note that each of these servants had a different starting position. Some of us start with a lot, and some of us don't. That unfairness is acknowledged in this story and is an excellent metaphor for women in the workplace or other leadership roles—our starting position may seem unfair as well.

> *It is not what you start with;*
> *it's what you do with it!*

The point is this: it is not what you start with; it's what you do with it! Two of the servants invested their talents and realized a gain. One dug a hole and buried his talent.

The successful servants in this story were not praised for being profitable. They were recognized for being faithful to what they had been given. The same is true for the many things women are given responsibility over. We may start with a disadvantage in terms of stereotypes, ceilings of glass, and built-in obstacles, but if we invest our talents wisely, we create a new position.

When the servant who hid his talent was called to account, he blamed the master! We live in a world that encourages and even rewards low accountability. Embracing accountability is empowering, but it may require a complete shift in the way we think about what accountability is.

What comes immediately to mind when you hear, "Who is accountable?"

Did you think of words like *responsibility* or *blame*? Accountability is often associated with blame. That's reasonable. Have you ever seen anyone run through the hallways at the office shouting, "Who's accountable?" when the news is good? I haven't. Normally when we go looking for who's accountable, we aren't measuring them for a medal.

In their book *The Oz Principle: Getting Results Through Individual and Organizational Accountability*, authors Roger Connors, Tom Smith, and Craig Hickman observe: "Somewhere along the line, society and organizations have stimulated people to feel more responsible for explaining results than for achieving them."[1]

The very moment I decide explanations and results are different, I distinguish myself. I move out of the Zone of Low Accountability and into the victim-free zone. Here I will be taken more seriously, build tremendous credibility, emerge with solutions instead of explanations, and adopt the powerful language of accountability.

The Zone of Low Accountability can be a very attractive place because excuses and explanations can be oh so comforting. We get to say, "It's not my fault," "No one told me," and "That's not my job."

We all go to the Zone of Low Accountability, and reading this book won't change that. It may be natural to go there. You just don't want to set up your tent and stay, because there you are powerless. The key is to quickly recognize when you have entered the zone and get yourself out of there!

It takes courage and resiliency to be accountable. It might mean admitting you have been wrong. Or it may require you to step out of a well-worn comfort zone. Accountability will eventually remind you that your skills are outdated and you need to upgrade. Accountability will cost you something, and it will pay you back in the most extraordinary ways.

Let's look at ways you can embrace and demonstrate personal accountability.

Ask the right questions.

When bad things happen, our first reaction may be, "Why?" or "Why me?" That may be the most natural response, but it will never be the most productive one.

It is absolutely true: if you ask the wrong question, you will get the wrong answer.

In his book *Flipping the Switch*, John G. Miller gives us some powerful and profound advice: "The answers are in the questions. When we ask better questions, we get better answers....It's important to remember that these are questions we ask of *ourselves*, not of others."[2]

Have you been to a blame-storming meeting? This is a meeting where we spend the entire time complaining about our situation and blaming something or someone else for it. These meetings frequently happen in the parking lot. People leave a blame-storming meeting exhausted and physically smaller, feeling powerless.

When circumstances are difficult, ask accountable questions. These are questions that redirect energies toward solutions, the future, and options. They sound like:

- What can I do?

- How am I contributing to the problem?

- How do I want this to turn out?

- What options are available?

Be a positive catalyst!

You can be the most positive catalyst in the workplace, at church, and at home. The next time you find yourself trapped in an exchange that has become a whine fest, be the one to step up and ask the accountable question.

When you hear a comment like "When is that person going to get their act together?" be the one to create a shift in thinking. You can ask, "What can we do to partner more effectively with this person?" or "How can we prevent this kind of communication breakdown from happening again?"

EMPOWER YOURSELF
THROUGH OPTIMISM

Negativity in almost every sphere and venue is an absolute epidemic. We all struggle against what feels like an ever-increasing tide of negativity; it literally weakens a church body, a career, or a team.

Negativity in a group has many sources. They include:

- Poor leadership

- Lack of recognition

- Rapid, disconnected change

- Limited resources

- Nonperforming members

- Constant pressure to do more with less

- Fear and uncertainty

- Poor communication

Even this short list is enough to depress anyone!

Studies confirm that the most successful people, careers, and organizations are marked by a relentless optimism. The most successful leaders are optimistic about the future. Even in the most challenging times, they never lose sight of their vision. Studies have even shown that optimistic workers increase their opportunities for advancement and have the potential to earn more.[3] Optimistic people present themselves with more confidence. They believe in their ability to overcome obstacles and achieve the goal. They are resilient and look to the future with expectancy.

The book *Good to Great* by Jim Collins is an extensive study on how a good company can become a great one. A common attribute of great organizations was "...the unwavering faith that [they would] prevail."[4] Collins found an unrelenting optimism in these great companies.

The difference between an optimist and a pessimist is the way they think about, talk about, and respond to setbacks.

We all have an explanation style—it's the way we interpret life events. In his book *Learned Optimism*, Dr. Martin Seligman presents the explanatory style as a habit of thinking.[5] Negativity is simply unchecked pessimism.

Your explanation is the sum of four factors: duration, orientation, responsibility, and scope. These four elements create DORS. And with every event, you will step through one of two DORS.

- *Duration* speaks to how long you think the event will last. For a pessimist, it will be forever! "This will *never* change. It will *always* be this way. We will *never* be the same." An optimist sees the same event differently. For the optimist, it is a temporary setback.

- *Orientation* is the direction you are looking. Pessimists look backward. They talk about what happened or didn't happen—what should have or shouldn't have occurred. Optimists look to the future. They talk about what needs to happen or what happens next.

- *Responsibility* reveals your focus or intention. Pessimists need to blame: "It's all your fault." "It's all my fault." The point is that someone must be blamed—and preferably punished. Optimists are not interested in blame. Their focus is on the solution. They want to fix the problem, not the blame.

- *Scope* tells us how much is impacted by this event. How big is this situation? Pessimists will tell you it is huge: "*Everything* is ruined. *Everyone* is upset.

Nothing is working the way it should."
Optimists isolate issues. They say, "This
is a problem," or "This isn't working the
way it should."

The explanation style is important, because how you explain an event determines how you respond to it. Optimism is a predictor of success for two reasons.

1. Those who learn this skill see themselves overcoming obstacles and crossing the finish line.

2. Those who see this skill in you see glimpses of leadership.

Responding to negativity in others

If you are serious about empowering yourself, breaking negative thought patterns, and learning optimism, you must be prepared to deal with negativity in others. This can be very hard for women because we are nurturing. We don't want to hurt anyone's feelings, we don't want to be rude, and we don't know how to tell this negative person they are sucking the life right out of us! So we listen and try to be supportive.

What begins as a shoulder to lean on and a listening ear can become very toxic. Before long we find ourselves knee-deep in the muck and drowning in the same attitude we tried to rescue.

You may work with or be close friends with someone right now who wants to whine and complain constantly. There are two reasons you need to stop this now. The first is guilt by association. Like it or not, your reputation and your credibility are damaged when you associate with negative people. We all need to take Jack Canfield's advice, "Avoid toxic people!"[6]

The second reason to take immediate action is the impact negativity has on your attitude and your productivity. When we participate in these "back-channel" conversations, we give our strength away. We weaken ourselves, our relationships, and our impact.

How do you shut off the tap of negativity and make yourself unavailable for that kind of communication? There are steps you can take to gracefully and firmly stop the negative flow.

1. Acknowledge what this person is feeling. It's OK to say, "I know you're very disappointed or discouraged."

2. Create a future focus: "How do you want this to turn out?" or "What needs to happen for you to feel better about this situation?"

3. Transition a conversation about problems to a conversation about solutions: "What

can you do to improve the outcome?
What are you willing to try?"

4. Offer options and alternatives: "What if
you were to...?" One of two things is
going to happen. Either you will help
someone who is stuck in a negative pattern, or this person won't come to you
anymore. Either of these outcomes is per-
fectly OK with me. Some people don't
want to be unstuck. They like sticking,
and they want you to stick with them.
My motto is: either fix it or forget it.

If you implement these steps and still find yourself
ambushed by negativity, you may need to become more
direct. That conversation sounds like, "I want to help
find solutions. Let's agree to talk about what you can
do to make it better—what you personally control. That
will empower you to make the necessary changes."

Chances are pretty slim that the negative people will
actually read this. When I speak on negativity, the negative people don't come—unless they are dragged! It's
the people trying to deal with the negative people who
actually show up. Just in case, if you are the negative
person, please stop! Your negativity is draining, and
the people who are trying to support you are tired of
holding you up.

EMPOWER YOURSELF WITH
PERSONAL RULES OF ENGAGEMENT

When communication becomes unproductive or conflicts arise, it is often because there are no established rules of engagement in place.

Your rules of engagement provide you with prearranged guidelines for how you handle conflict, manage sensitive or confidential information, and communicate. I encourage you to set boundaries and protect your trustworthiness with a personal set of operating agreements.

Here are a few examples of communication ground rules that foster loyalty, build trust, and empower you.

1. I am loyal to the person who isn't in the room.[7]

2. I speak to issues, not about them—to people, not about them.

3. I talk about what I can impact.

4. My conversations are solutions oriented.

5. I am committed to productive communication, and I ask for the same in return.

Rules of engagement are good guides. They keep you on track. They are also good teachers. When someone comes to you with the latest juicy gossip about Susie in accounts payable, you simply say, "Wait! I have this communication rule about being loyal to the person who isn't in the room. I want to hear every juicy detail of your story. Please wait here while I go get her!"

The gossip won't be there when you return, and she won't bring you her communication trash again.

When you consider the stereotypes already in place—you know the notions about women being catty, gossipy, and dependent—these rules aren't an option. Without them we risk falling right into those roles and reinforcing those assumptions!

EMPOWER YOURSELF WITH SPIRITUAL DISCIPLINE

The most successful, satisfied women I know empower themselves with disciplines that support their purpose and vision. One of my mentors puts it this way, "Make sure your rituals sustain your values and vision."

What are your daily rituals? (I promise you have some. If you're like me, a closer look will reveal some that are empowering and some that are limiting.) Your rituals are your routines. They include your spiritual goals, how you begin and end the day, the appointments you keep for the things that touch the heart of God, what you focus on, and how you purposefully and consistently climb to a higher place in your faith.

I've found that spiritual disciplines mirror time management strategies in some ways. I want to be proactive spiritually. That means devoting time for the things that grow me up and fill me up. My life works best when I honor these appointments. When I am feeling unbalanced or reactive, I know it's time to inventory my routines.

CHAPTER 3

Grow Your Emotional Intelligence

Laugh with your happy friends when they're happy; share tears when they're down. Get along with each other; don't be stuck-up. Make friends with nobodies; don't be the great somebody.

—ROMANS 12:15

AWARENESS IS ESSENTIAL to surviving and thriving. This has always been true, and never more so than in today's world. The rules and expectations are changing. There is constant pressure to do more with less. Competition is fierce, and the race to innovation is accelerating. The challenge is enormous. The opportunity is amazing.

Do an Internet search on the word *awareness*, and

you'll find hundreds of awareness campaigns. These causes promote early detection, prevention, and understanding. That's very appropriate for your cause as well. For the powerful woman of God, awareness is a key concept.

At the cornerstone of awareness are the emotional intelligence (EI) competencies. We call them competencies because they can be learned. That's exciting because these competencies account for greater percentages of success in every walk of life.

Emotional intelligence gives IQ impact.

In the workplace there is often a focus—sometimes even an arrogance—around technical competencies. Technical skills are certainly important, but we are beginning to understand those skills don't stand well alone. We've all met people who are highly educated, very intelligent, or are blessed with amazing spiritual gifts, but they can't communicate their way out of a paper bag! All of that knowledge, intelligence, and gifting are mute if we can't connect with people in a meaningful way.

So the scorecards are in, and people with high emotional intelligence win. Emotional intelligence gives

IQ impact. It determines the level of relationship, and relationship determines the level of result.

WHAT IS EMOTIONAL INTELLIGENCE?

Emotional intelligence is a set of intuitive skills. You may not even be aware when you are using them. These skills include confidence, perseverance, empathy, enthusiasm, and self-motivation. If you can make these a more conscious choice, you give yourself more control. In that way, emotional intelligence is awareness. Increase your EI by increasing your awareness on many levels.

In the book *The EQ Difference*, Adele B. Lynn calls emotional intelligence your "inner bird dog."[1] People with high emotional intelligence have internalized a set of skills allowing them to be centered and poised even in the most difficult situations. We are drawn to people with high emotional intelligence. We are attracted to their confidence and how we feel when we are with them. We connect with these people because they understand us. These people read situations differently. They see things others don't—intuitively understanding what others miss.

People with high emotional intelligence:[2]

- *Recognize what they are feeling and why.* They understand the impact of their emotions on relationships and results.

- *Assess themselves accurately.* They are aware of their strengths and weaknesses. They seek feedback and use it to grow.

- *Are confident and self-assured.* They are decisive and can stand alone if necessary.

- *Demonstrate focus and self-control.* They manage impulses and remain composed even in difficult, stressful situations.

- *Build trust*—through authenticity and integrity.

- *Take responsibility.* They hold themselves accountable.

- *Adapt.* They flex with multiple demands, change, and shifting priorities.

- *Innovate.* They are open to new approaches and ideas; they seek fresh perspectives.

- *Are self-motivated.* These are results-oriented people with a strong drive for performance and excellence.

- *Are deeply committed* to the goals of their family, group, or organization.

- *Take extreme initiative.* They exceed expectations.

- *Operate from an optimistic frame.* They persist in the face of adversity and setbacks.

- *Empathize with others*—listen between the words.

- *Have a service orientation.* They know how to meet people's needs and create loyalty.

- *Develop and encourage others*—through recognition, feedback, and challenge.

- *See diversity as an opportunity* to leverage different backgrounds and perspectives.

- *Understand the politics*—the social networks and forces that shape perspectives and behaviors.

- *Influence others.* They are persuasive—able to build consensus and support.

- *Communicate effectively.* They give and receive information well. They reach for a deeper understanding and create open dialogue.

- *Inspire people* with a compelling vision.

- *Initiate change* and challenge the status quo.

- *Manage conflict and negotiate effectively.* They design win-win outcomes.

- *Build a network of strong relationships.*

- *Invite collaboration* and work with others to achieve shared goals.

- *Create team performance and identity.*

Before reading on, review the list again. With this description in mind, who is your emotional intelligence role model? Who in your life or work embodies these attributes and skills? How many of these statements describe you? Which ones do you need to work on?

Emotional Intelligence Begins With Self-Awareness

The best news about emotional intelligence is that you can have more. In fact, you can have as much as you want. The only catch is that to have more EI, you must have more awareness, and that begins with self.

The first goal is to be more aware of our responses, reactions, and needs. As this awareness grows, we are able to develop objective-based responses.

On their own, emotions make terrible drivers, bad guides, and worse decision makers. Emotions will hijack you if you let them. They will pick you up and carry you off! When the ride is over, you may find yourself further from your goals and intentions. I have learned it is a long walk home.

This can be a huge problem for women in positions of influence. We are already labeled as emotional, needy, and irrational. When we allow emotions to drive the car, we perpetuate the stereotypes and drive us even further from the recognition we wanted.

We can consciously rein in our emotions by asking a new set of questions:

- How am I feeling?

- Why am I feeling that way?

- What do I need?

- What am I afraid will happen?

- How do I want this to turn out?

- What can I do to achieve the result I need?

The moment you begin this self-inquiry, a switch flips in your brain. You are moving from a purely emotional response to an objective-based response.

Instead of being packed off by our emotions, we can teach objectives to drive. We can learn to ask new questions of ourselves, tell ourselves the truth, and take conscious, deliberate steps in the direction of our goal.

BECOME MORE SELF-AWARE THROUGH CONSTRUCTIVE FEEDBACK

Self-awareness comes from other sources as well. If we allow it, feedback can be a marvelous tool. A dear colleague and friend of mine sometimes says, "Feedback is a gift, and boy, do I have a present for you!"

Feedback is all around you. It is in what people say or don't say. It is in facial expressions and body language. It's in the cooperation or resistance you encounter. There is feedback in the way your ideas are received and the questions you are asked.

Emotional intelligence is marked by accurate self-assessment—knowing one's strengths and weaknesses. Have you met someone who is painfully unaware of how badly they come across to others—demanding, defensive, argumentative, or inappropriate? What is the cost of this low awareness? How much time and energy do they spend overcoming the resistance of their own making? How much are their relationships damaged? What opportunities do they forfeit?

Yes, feedback is a gift. When you stop and think about it, it is just ludicrous to sit back and passively wait for another person to tell you how you are affecting them. Instead of waiting, initiate a dialogue. Ask for feedback. This can happen at work as well. Don't wait around for your once- or twice-a-year performance review. The performance is yours, and so is the feedback. Go get it! It will make you better.

Here are some questions you can use to get the conversation moving:

- What do you see as my greatest strengths?

- Where would you like to see greater effort?

- What do I need to do to be more effective?

- Where do you wish I would spend more time? Less time?

- How can I have a more positive impact here?

- How can I become more valuable to you?

Questions like this are not for the fainthearted, but they are irresistible! Imagine someone asking these questions of you. What impression would you have of a person who is this interested in being the best they can possibly be?

When I ask managers what they would think of an employee who calls a meeting to initiate this kind of conversation, I hear a unanimous, "Wow!" Most managers then say this has never, ever happened to them.

Several positive things are triggered when you have the courage to ask for feedback. It's disarming and solutions based. If there is tension or you sense there's a problem, asking for feedback allows you to isolate the issues so you can do something about them. You demonstrate maturity and personal accountability. You called the meeting, so you get to drive the agenda! And above all, it immediately sets you apart from everyone who isn't proactively managing their feedback.

Get ready. Hang on. You will hear some things you don't like—things you don't agree with. You may be tempted to argue about your feedback or explain yourself. *Resist that temptation with all of your might!*

When you receive feedback, simply say, "Thank you."

That doesn't mean you agree with everything that has been said. It simply means you appreciate the honesty. Later you can decide how to use the feedback or, if you disagree, how to manage the perception you have discovered.

As you search for feedback, keep it in perspective. The feedback you receive isn't necessarily who you are. It doesn't define or limit you. It is a perception. In order to manage perceptions, you must understand what they are and how they are created.

> Amanda is young and aggressive. She has been identified as high potential and participates in the organization's mentoring program. She is opinionated and outspoken. Unfortunately, most of her contributions are negative. She argues insignificant points and regularly positions herself on the opposite side of discussions.
>
> Honestly? She wears me out, and I told her so.
>
> She was shocked to learn that I found her to be distracting and counterproductive. She thought of herself as edgy and thought provoking—an independent thinker, challenging the status quo.
>
> I encouraged Amanda not to take my word for it. After all, mine is just one perception. I challenged her to closely monitor the reactions and responses of her colleagues, gather additional feedback, and decide for herself if changes were warranted.
>
> About a month later I saw Amanda again. The transformation was incredible! She was still outspoken, but in a productive way. When I congratulated her on the adjustment she had obviously made, she had a confession to make.

She said, "When you gave me the feedback, I was very angry—first with you and later with myself. I pouted for a few days. I decided to punish everyone by not saying anything at all. When I finally came around, I realized I wasn't having the impact I want to have on this group. I want to be known for initiating change, not conflict. I've asked a few of my colleagues to give me feedback on the adjustments I'm making, and I notice people responding to my ideas more positively."

I love the honesty in that! Amanda received difficult feedback. She processed the data emotionally for a minute, and then she used the feedback to make positive changes. When she asked her peers to help monitor her progress, she took the feedback to a whole new level. She owned it.

If you take charge of your feedback and use it to make you better, you'll enhance your emotional intelligence and be a positive force in people's lives.

Go get your gift and open it early!

INCREASE YOUR
AWARENESS OF OTHERS

On the next level, we become more aware of others. This awareness of others allows us to leverage diversity as a distinct set of relationship skills. We reach for a deeper understanding, challenging our perceptions and assumptions. We learn how to bring the best out in others.

One of my dearest friends and a member of my "extended family" is a master at bringing out the best in others. She looks below the behavior to find what is driving it. She reaches beneath what is unattractive— even obnoxious—to find a glimpse of good. Then she focuses on that goodness. The amazing thing is how people respond to her. By focusing on what is good in people, she brings it to the surface!

Our awareness of others—our ability to understand and connect in a meaningful way—is constrained by pre-conceived notions, assumptions, perceptions, and labels.

CHECK THE LABELS

We all label people. It is our way of organizing, arranging, and categorizing. We put stuff—even people—in neat little boxes with labels attached to remind us what's inside. What is worse than the labels we slap on people is the behavior it evokes.

Labels become filters that we listen through, and they can actually reinforce themselves. This is a bit like chickens and eggs. Which came first, the label or the behavior?

Let's say I work with you, and I have labeled you as "defensive." I need to speak with you about something today. It's not a big deal, but you will make it a big deal—because that's what defensive people do.

As I approach you, I am ready for a defensive response. My posture is tense and rigid. My father used to call this stance "loaded for bear."

What does that look like to you? An attack! You see me coming—loaded for bear—and you prepare to defend yourself. We have our encounter, and it does become argumentative and confrontational. I walk away, shaking my head, saying to myself how defensive and obnoxious you are.

What just happened? First I labeled you. Then I reached into the situation, pulled out a defensive response, and judged you for it! How convenient is that?

Years ago while traveling in England, I ran across a book called *Miller's Bolt* by Thomas Stirr.[3] It is a wonderful book—a business parable—about building and rebuilding professional relationships. Inside the story is an exercise that I found fascinating and rewarding. I'd like to share it with you.

Think of someone you have a difficult time communicating with and relating to. This is someone you need to communicate with frequently and a relationship you care about. If you don't care about the person or the relationship, skip this exercise. It won't work.

Once you have this person in mind, write down three words describing them. Chances are the words that come immediately to mind won't be a glowing report.

The words you have written down are the labels you have virtually pasted to the forehead of this difficult person. This is the box you have put them in. Every communication must pass through this filter; you are actually responding to the label, not the person.

For the communication to change, the filter must change. You must reach for a deeper understanding. Do that by neutralizing the negative filter.

In some cases, it's easy to neutralize or even find a positive aspect to the label. "Picky" might become "detail oriented." "Pushy" in a more positive frame could be "direct." Sometimes it is harder to reframe the behavior.

Let's say I am having trouble with my boss; I describe her as a "control freak." How do I neutralize that? I may need to reach below the behavior to the cause. What causes a person to over control? It is fear. My boss is afraid. When I remove the "control freak" label and replace it with "afraid," something marvelous happens. I will respond differently to someone who is afraid.

Labels box us in. When I manage the labels effectively, I release others from the box and allow (even invite) a new and more productive pattern of communication.

One of the demonstrations I frequently use in leadership workshops is uncanny—almost frightening, actually. I select five participants from the audience and ask them to step up to the front of the room. Here, five chairs are arranged.

I place a hat on each volunteer. On each hat is a label. One of the volunteers is labeled a leader. Others are labeled negative, people pleaser, and lazy. The last volunteer is labeled invisible. The volunteers can see the labels on each other, but they do not know what their own label is.

They are told they have been chosen to serve on a special committee. The goal of this group is to recommend ways to improve group motivation and morale. They are instructed to meet now for ten minutes to discuss ideas and draft a plan. The only rule is they must respond to the labels of the other members on the committee.

No matter what is said, they are to use the labels to formulate their response. I then turn to the volunteer labeled as leader and ask this person to lead the meeting. She looks a little surprised initially, but she quickly steps into the role. Each time the leader speaks, the room agrees. We hang on to every word. The other volunteers direct their comments and ideas to the leader. Within minutes the leader is sitting taller and taking charge. She is acting like a leader. Why? Because she is being treated like one!

Remember the invisible volunteer? Each time she speaks, she is ignored. She is interrupted and her ideas are discounted. Very quickly she shuts down. She says nothing and stares at the floor. She has indeed become invisible.

This exercise teaches us that we can bring out the best or the worst in others. People with high EI purposefully and deliberately bring out the best.

The exercise also reminds us that we are all carrying labels—like those name tags they slap on you at conferences. While we don't always know what the labels say, they are inspiring responses from others. They are the context for communication.

LOOK BEYOND THE SURFACE

In *The Seven Habits of Highly Effective People*, Dr. Stephen Covey teaches, "Seek first to understand, then to be understood."[4] This is a ground rule for empathy.

Empathy is simply the willingness to try to understand how another feels. It is not agreement. It is reaching for a deeper understanding.

> I learned about empathy from a young woman at the Dallas/Fort Worth International Airport. I was making a connection on my way to Boston when a huge thunderstorm brought everything to a grinding halt. Connections were lost, and the travel nightmare began. Situations like this do not bring the best out in people.
>
> I found myself in the dreaded customer service line. This, by the way, is an oxymoron. There

should be no line in customer service. This long line was weaving through the concourse, and the people in it were grumpy. They were taking their frustrations out on the young woman behind the counter. She, on the other hand, was doing a marvelous job of provoking everyone—she was horrible really.

I do believe in objective-based communication and immediately found my objective. I was going to make her cry. It was a public service really.

With that goal in mind I began preparing my speech, and it was coming together beautifully. When my turn finally came, I stepped up to the counter ready to unleash the lecture guaranteed to put this rude woman in her place. That is when I remembered the real goal. Get to Boston. I had wasted my waiting time preparing for the wrong objective!

In that split second the only thing I could think of was to empathize. So I did. I said to her, "I cannot imagine how it must feel to stand behind that counter with a hundred people waiting to yell at me." She burst into tears. It was one of the finest moments of my life.

Then she taught me something I will never forget. She said, "I don't control the weather. I don't control when the planes come or when they go. I do control who sits on them and where. In situations like this, I try to save a seat in first class for the person who is kind."

I sat in that seat—4B, to be exact.

I learned empathy is powerful. It quite literally gets you where you need to go. And that's not the end of my lesson. When I began to try to understand how she might be feeling behind that counter, I didn't see a rude gate agent. I saw a young woman without the skills, tools, or support she needed to deal with the situation she was in. I still did not agree with her behavior, but I could understand it. I could even relate to it. I've been there.

When I stood in judgment of her, she was the enemy. Empathy opened a door of understanding and created a whole new possibility— and a seat in first class.

DEVELOP A SENSE FOR
THE SITUATION

When we step into the level of developing a sense for a particular situation, we are in the moment and keenly aware of the circumstances. We understand the undercurrents, hidden agendas, and sensitivities. We read between the lines and hear what isn't said. And we think about the stakeholders and the stakes—understanding what people have, or perceive, to gain or to lose.

Consider Chris, who was asked by her boss to review a set of procedures and make recommendations to improve them. This was right up her alley—a definite strength. She set about evaluating the procedures and found them cumbersome and redundant.

In a staff meeting, she mentioned her work on the procedures and let the group know how much easier the new process would be for them. Chris thought she was bringing good news to her hardworking colleagues, and she expected them to be relieved and grateful.

An awkward silence filled the room. Chris didn't realize the original authors of the procedure were sitting in that meeting. To them, her good news was like cold water in the face.

Situational awareness protects us from stepping in something or stomping on toes. Think of it like the ridges on the sides of a freeway lane. If you run over those, you certainly know it. They alert you—you've edged out of your lane. Correct your course!

USE AWARENESS TO ANTICIPATE THE FUTURE

Anticipatory awareness is readiness. Readiness is difficult because it is easy to become very task oriented and to lose sight of the big picture. We develop anticipatory awareness or readiness by continually asking, "What's next?"

Columnist George F. Will once wrote, "The future has a way of arriving unannounced." Change is certain.

If we don't recognize and respond to change, we risk becoming outdated, stagnant, and ineffective. This ability to change is the combination of two factors—awareness and ability. When you add those pieces together, you get change-ability. To grow and thrive in the future, we must increase our change-ability.

When faced with the realization that the future has arrived, and they weren't ready for it, people often say, "Why didn't we see this coming?" The answer is simple: "We weren't searching for it. We didn't ask the right questions. We let ourselves get comfortable."

I like the advice from Jack Welch when he said, "Change before you have to."

Incidentally, whether you are a leader or a member of a team, anticipatory awareness is an essential skill. This kind of thinking isn't reserved for ivory towers, boardrooms, and executive retreats. The moment you begin thinking like this, you become more valuable to the group you serve.

Problems and challenges are excellent change detectors. These are red flags waving in the wind, telling you something must change!

Just like communication, awareness is also an inside-out job. It starts with self-awareness and ultimately becomes our connection with the future. These emotional intelligence skills give us more control and flexibility—they become keys that unlock our possibilities.

CHAPTER 4

Ask for What You Want

She asked permission. "Let me glean," she said, "and gather among the sheaves following after your harvesters."... Boaz ordered his servants: "Let her glean where there's still plenty of grain on the ground—make it easy for her....Give her special treatment."

—RUTH 2:7–16

AUTHORS LINDA BABCOCK and Sara Laschever discuss how women feel about negotiation and the price of their reluctance in the book *Women Don't Ask: Negotiation and the Gender Divide*.[1] From their research we learn:

- Women are four times less likely than men to initiate negotiations and more than twice as apprehensive about it.

- Men describe negotiating as a competition, like winning a ball game, while women think of it as a trip to the dentist.

- Women pay more for purchases to avoid negotiating.

- Men ask for more when negotiating; women ask for less. Even when they do negotiate, women believe less is available.

- Negotiating a starting salary makes a significant difference. Women who consistently negotiate earn at least $1 million more during their careers than women who don't.

- Women tend to undervalue their worth.

We won't always get what we ask for, and some of our negotiations will fail. That doesn't mean we should quit trying!

> Sometimes we may feel like the woman in a recent workshop who said, "I don't speak up anymore. It doesn't do any good. I've learned to just do what they tell me."
>
> Her whole demeanor was one of defeat and resignation—tired of the battle. A robot now, she simply follows orders. She has learned the wrong lesson from her negotiation experiences!

In the Bible, we are encouraged to ask and to keep asking: "Keep on asking, and you will receive what you ask for. Keep on seeking, and you will find. Keep on knocking, and the door will be opened to you" (Matthew 7:7, NLT).

The resiliency to keep asking may require us to change our approach—how we are asking. We may need to rethink what we're asking for, prepare more thoroughly, offer evidence, anticipate objections, consider other perspectives, and suggest alternatives.

When our negotiations fail, we may need to gracefully accept that and move on. Walking around with a giant chip on your shoulder is exhausting, unattractive, and very bad for posture. But a failed negotiation—or two or three or ten—doesn't mean we stop asking altogether.

In the example above, this woman stopped asking because it didn't seem to make a difference. In other cases, perhaps we don't even know what to ask for—we haven't clearly identified what we need. Sometimes we may not ask because deep down we believe we should be able to do it all without help. In that light, asking for help means we haven't done "our job." Perhaps the most tragic reason of all is we don't ask because we don't think we deserve.

*Negotiation is a reasonable
exchange of value, not a matter
of winning or losing.*

Before we are free to ask, we may need to put a different frame around negotiation. Women often see negotiation as conflict or a fight. We don't like conflict, and we don't like to fight. That can make even the thought of negotiation agonizing.

What if you thought of negotiation as collaboration—the opportunity to explore alternatives and create more value for everyone involved? What if you saw negotiation as a creative, problem-solving process designed to explore less obvious solutions?

Perhaps one of the best ways to reframe negotiation is to think about what we give up when we don't negotiate and what we might gain if we do. A simple cost/benefit analysis may be in order.

Negotiation isn't just about money or even something you do only in the workplace. We can also negotiate for the things that make us worth more and our lives more satisfying. Here's a short list of what we can—and should—negotiate for:

1. More challenging responsibility

2. More rewarding assignments

3. More authority

4. Greater flexibility or control in the way
   you do your job

5. Training and professional development

6. Resources and tools

7. Help from spouse or children
   with household duties and other
   responsibilities

The benefits of negotiating are obvious. We get more of what we want and need more often. When we fail to negotiate, we set others and ourselves up for disappointment.

> Tammy works for a bank. She is an excellent salesperson, and her boss involves her in special business-development projects. As a result, she is often asked to work long and nontraditional hours. Tammy doesn't claim overtime or even keep track of these extra hours for two reasons: being asked feels like recognition, and she doesn't know how to bring it up. This pattern continues for about a year. Tammy is beginning to resent the amount of unpaid time she is working, and she resents her boss for taking such advantage of her.

When we fail to negotiate, it's possible, even likely, we will eventually feel taken advantage of. When that happens, we may "blame" our family or the organization we serve.

> *Ask without apology and with the
> expectation of getting what you ask for.*

Ironically, some of the best negotiators I know are women. When I think about what sets them apart, they are very confident and knowledgeable. They ask without apology and with the expectation of getting what they ask for. Maybe the greatest difference is in how they feel about negotiating and what they believe it is. First, they believe everything is negotiable—they see options and alternatives others miss. Next, they see negotiation as a reasonable exchange of value. They don't think of negotiation as winning or losing.

Let's compare that with what is probably more typical.

Elizabeth is a Realtor in Seattle. She is hard-working, patient, and completely committed to her clients. We can learn a great deal from the negotiating lessons she learned—the hard way—early in her career.

"My clients were first-time home buyers," Elizabeth explains, "and I worked with them for six long months. They had a lot to learn, and so did I. After viewing dozens of homes, they found the perfect one. Then we promptly lost it in the negotiation.

"The home was older, and the inspection came in with a lengthy list of repairs. Some of these repairs were essential; others were recommendations and minor issues. After reviewing the inspection report with my clients, I asked them, 'What do you want the sellers to repair?' The clients said, 'Everything. We want them to fix everything.'

"Dutifully I went back to the sellers with the message. Visibly wincing I said, 'My buyers want you to repair everything noted in the inspection.' The sellers were stunned by what they felt was completely unreasonable. They simply replied, 'We have a backup offer on the house, and we're going to take it.' Game over.

"At first I was so frustrated—and more than a little angry with my clients for being so unreasonable. Then it hit me. Not only had I failed to negotiate, I didn't even realize I was in a negotiation! I let myself become a messenger in the transaction—like a school girl passing notes in class!"

In this situation there were two negotiations happening simultaneously, and Elizabeth missed both of them. She failed to negotiate the inspection report with her own clients to reset their expectations and create a reasonable bottom line.

And she failed to negotiate with the sellers to close the deal.

You may be thinking, "She's a Realtor, for heaven's sake. Her job is to negotiate!" That may be true, but can you relate to her experience?

- Have you ever missed an opportunity to negotiate?

- Have you ever paid too much or settled for not enough?

- Has your hard work ever been wasted because you weren't clear on your bottom line?

- Have you ever said yes when you should have said no?

- Have you ever agreed to something that you wished you hadn't?

- Have you walked away feeling as if you gave a whole lot more than you received?

We can't be too hard on Elizabeth. She teaches us that even in jobs where negotiation is an assumed skill, it's not an automatic one.

Elizabeth's negotiating lessons weren't finished. She still needed to learn the importance of creating a win-win. "I was so eager to please," she admits. "In one very memorable transaction, I proudly brought the sellers a full-price offer and a commitment from my client to close in record time.

"The sellers were thrilled. They thought I was a miracle worker. But when I went back to my client with the accepted offer, he said, 'Let me see if I understand: We are offering full price for this home *and* agreeing to close practically tomorrow. What exactly did I get in return for that?'"

Elizabeth did not have an answer. She had agreed to give extra value with a quick close, but she had not asked for anything in return. "The closing was very stressful because we had agreed on such a short time frame. My client was stomping mad every step of the way. He did not feel like he 'won' anything in the negotiation, and he reminded me of that daily."

The best negotiations are the ones in which everyone feels like a winner.

Where Logic and Emotion Meet

Inside every negotiation, two processes are at work: the psychological or emotional process, and the rational or logical process.[2]

Emotional (Psychological) Process	Logical (Rational) Process
How comfortable we are in the negotiation	Analyzing the situation—critical thinking
What we assume about this situation and our chances of success	Generating options and alternatives—creative thinking
How much we trust the others involved	Problem solving
What we perceive is at stake—what is to lose and what is to gain	Decision making

If there is a weakness on either side of this process, negotiations will suffer. I may be extremely comfortable in the negotiation, but if I fail to analyze the situation, I weaken my ability to negotiate substantially.

If we return to Elizabeth and the failed real-estate transaction, we can see breakdowns in both the emotional and the logical processes. Elizabeth wasn't confident in her negotiating role, and she didn't work with her clients to generate options and alternatives to creatively solve the problem. She came to the table with an ultimatum and discovered her clients had viable alternatives!

KNOW WHAT YOU CAN'T
LIVE WITHOUT

Go into every negotiation knowing exactly what you want, knowing what you can't leave without, and knowing what your options are if the negotiations fail.

In the book *Getting to Yes: Negotiating Agreement Without Giving In*, authors Roger Fisher and William Ury give us the tool BATNA. Your BATNA is your "best alternative to a negotiated agreement."[3]

Think of your BATNA as a ruler, negotiation guide, or measuring stick. This ruler gives you the confidence to decide whether to accept or reject what is offered because you know what your alternatives are if you don't. When you are very clear about your alternatives, you protect yourself from agreeing to something that isn't in your best interest or rejecting terms that may be.

Using best alternatives as a guide, the general rule is to accept terms that are better than your BATNA and try to renegotiate terms that are not. Strengthen your negotiating position by strengthening your options.

That just means more and better alternatives give you a stronger negotiating position.

Skilled negotiators also consider the options of others involved.

Skilled negotiators also consider the options of others involved. What alternatives do they have if negotiations with you fail? The following case illustrates how important it is to understand the alternatives.

Diane is a senior loan processor for a mortgage company. She has been with her firm for ten years. A competitor has offered her a 10 percent increase in salary. Today she met with her boss to ask for a 10 percent raise.

Diane's best alternative is very strong. If she doesn't receive the raise she is asking for, she can resign and take the job offer. Using that as a guide, anything less than a 10 percent pay increase is unfavorable.

Diane's boss appears to have weaker alternatives. If she loses one of her most senior processors, she may have to replace the talent. That will impact productivity and service consistency; it will cost money. Unless she can improve her options, granting Diane's request may be the wise choice.

But what if options do exist? What if volume projections are down and Diane's boss can absorb the loss of a processor? Perhaps she can replace one senior processor with two junior processors and increase processing capacity. With these alternatives, perhaps she doesn't agree to the increase.

On the surface of this negotiation, the choices seem limited. Diane will either receive a raise or leave the company. Her boss will either grant the request or lose a valuable employee. These are win-lose or lose-win outcomes. How can these women create a win-win alternative?

MAKE THE PIE BIGGER

In negotiations there are two distinct strategies: distributive bargaining (claiming value) and integrative bargaining (creating value).[4]

Distributive bargaining is a win-lose strategy. Resources are generally fixed, and sides compete for pieces of the pie. With this strategy, each side of the negotiation is primarily concerned with maximizing its own interests—getting more of the pie—and claiming more value.

When distributive bargaining is used, negotiation tactics may include power plays like manipulation, force, and withholding information. Cards are held close to the chest, and the other side of the negotiation is considered the enemy. Here negotiation is a competition. There is one pie, and the goal is to get more pieces of it.

With integrative or collaborative bargaining, it is possible for both sides to win. In fact, that is the goal. We believe we can make the pie bigger. We can create more value. Sides are primarily concerned with maximizing joint interests, and tactics include information sharing, collaboration, brainstorming, and creative problem solving.

The real question becomes, "How can we both get more of what we want and need in this situation?" Rather than an adversary, the other side becomes a problem-solving partner.

Distributive (Competitive) Bargaining Strategies	Integrative (Collaborative) Bargaining Strategies
The first offer is an "anchor" and sets the bargaining range. Come in high!	Share information about your circumstances.
Do not disclose significant information about your circumstances.	Work to understand what is important to others involved. What are their primary concerns, hopes, fears, or objectives?

Distributive (Competitive) Bargaining Strategies	Integrative (Collaborative) Bargaining Strategies
Don't let the other side see a weakness.	Explain what is important to you, and why.
Make it clear you have other options.	Discuss preferences and options openly.
Let them know you can, and may, walk at any time.	Talk about ways you can add more value to the deal.

Integrative bargaining uses disclosure to connect with the needs and goals of everyone involved. It openly invites collaboration. Picture yourself moving to the same side of the table—partnering to find a solution that meets the primary interests of both sides. You may even declare it! You might say, "I want to understand your goals here. I want us to find a solution that works for both of us." (Yes, you can say this to your two-year-old. They understand good bargaining options as well as anyone.)

Sometimes we can create more value in our negotiations by offering something we value less in exchange for something we value more. Think about the case of the employee we risk losing. What are some things

Diane's boss could throw in? What might her senior processor greatly value that she can afford to give away?

Diane's manager may be unable to offer a 10 percent increase. Perhaps she can only offer 5 percent. Or she might make the pie bigger by offering:

- An additional week of paid vacation

- Specialized training

- A more flexible schedule

- The visibility and recognition of working on a strategic team to improve processes

Diane's boss needs to make this negotiation more than a discussion about money. If she views this as a problem to solve *with* her employee, she can turn it into collaboration.

WHEN YOU GIVE VALUE, SAY SO

By the way, when you give something in a negotiation, make sure the other side knows they are receiving real value.

> I learned this from watching Liz, a successful entrepreneur who has built a thriving training company. When she throws something into the deal to add value, she candidly tells the client, "I

am giving you something here. It has real value,
and I'm giving it to you."

If you give something away without declaring the
value, you may create an unrealistic expectation for
future negotiations. Instead of creating value you
can draw on, you have created the expectation for
accommodation.

---

*Women can be great negotiators
because we are relationship
oriented and collaborative.*

THE ENEMIES OF COLLABORATION

Women can be great negotiators because we are relationship oriented and collaborative. These are often
natural skills. We are good at connecting with what is
important to others, but collaboration does have ene-
mies. It is impossible to invite a spirit of collaboration
when we:

- Defend positions rather than work to
  understand interests

- Fail to locate what matters most to
  everyone involved

- Are overly concerned with the needs of others at the expense of our own needs—that's not negotiation, that's accommodation

- Assume someone must win and someone must lose

- Allow emotions to dominate the process

- Let it get personal

To demonstrate the dynamics of collaboration, I often ask audience members to "choose a partner; move anything that will spill, break, or hurt you; and prepare to arm wrestle!" With a groan, they move into position. Next I tell them they have twelve seconds to win. In fact, I want them to win as often as they can in the time allowed. To spur them on, I ask them to pretend they will receive $1,000 each time they win.

The transformation is amazing! The gentlest of people become the fiercest of contenders. Even in this pretend negotiation, everyone wants to win! The twelve seconds are a complete frenzy. Some people are winning, some are losing, and some pairs are strained in a red-faced draw. When I call time, some don't want to quit because there has been no winner.

When I ask for the winners to stand, they do so proudly. Some of them have pummeled their partners repeatedly, and they are quite pleased with themselves—until they hear the true solution.

What if you didn't see this as a win-or-lose situation? What if you had collaborated with your partner? What if you had asked, "How can we both win more?"

The solution is simple. Let's not resist each other. I will let you win and you will let me win. We will do that as fast as we can—arms flying back and forth for twelve seconds. Another groan fills the room as people realize they completely missed the opportunity to win more by competing less.

FOCUS ON WHY RATHER THAN WHAT

In negotiation, your position is what you want. Your interests are why you want that—why it matters to you. It is the underlying need. If you focus primarily on positions in a negotiation—what you want or what others want—you limit the possibilities tremendously. You box yourself in and set yourself up for a win-lose or lose-win situation.

Seasoned negotiators look for integrative solutions, and those can be found by understanding the interests of everyone involved.

As you build your negotiation skills, you will learn

people are people after all, and they are essentially concerned with, interested in, and looking for the same things you are. Remember Abraham Maslow's hierarchy of needs? He contended that once our basic needs are met, we look for ways to be more secure, then to belong, then to achieve, and finally to reach our fullest potential.[5]

This can be a useful model when you think about what motivates people in a negotiation. If I am worried about enough money to pay my bills, that need will drive me. Once that need is met, other things may become more important to me—the need for recognition, challenge, and achievement.

In our sample case, Diane's position is a 10 percent raise. That is what she wants. But do we really know why?

Maybe Diane wants to earn more or maybe she *needs* to earn more. Something may have changed in her life, causing a financial strain. Perhaps the money is not the issue at all—the real need is to feel more valued and recognized. Maybe after ten years with the company she believes she has capped out financially. There is no room for her to grow—to reach her full potential.

Diane's position is clear: she wants a raise. Before meeting with Diane, her boss would be wise to consider the underlying interests, develop a plan to discover what is most important to her, and look for integrative solutions—a win for the organization and a win for Diane.

DISCOVER WHAT MATTERS MOST

As you prepare to negotiate, you can make some assumptions about what is important to the others involved. As you begin to negotiate, you will want to verify, clarify, and invite people to talk about what matters most. Equip yourself with questions:

- What is your primary concern?

- What is most important to you?

- Why is this so important to you?

Ultimately, negotiation is about creating and exchanging value. These are also the instruments of influence. In the book *Influence Without Authority*, Allan Cohen and David Bradford frame influence as exchange. There is something you need or want, and you must find something of value to trade for it.[6] The Law of Reciprocity is at work here.

When we give something of value, people are more inclined to give something of value in return. Before you ask for something in a negotiation, consider what you have to give.

> Kathy, an incredible Realtor in South Texas, intuitively understands the Law of Reciprocity. She was negotiating a large transaction with an attorney. When he asked her which title

company she would be using, she immediately recognized an opportunity to give. She said, "If you have someone you would like to give this business to, let's go with that firm. This may be a good way for you to build or strengthen that relationship."

The attorney was grateful. He did have someone in mind—someone who had just referred business to him. This was his opportunity to return the favor. Then Kathy asked for something in return—a big something actually.

Without batting an eye, she asked, "Who will be paying for the title policy?" I'll let you guess who picked up that bill.

What you have to give is your currency. And most of us have more currency and more kinds of currency than we may realize.

Find your currencies by thinking about what you have to offer. Do you have specialized knowledge, information, or skills? Can you give appreciation, support, recognition, or visibility? Do you have contacts or other resources you can share? From time to time it's worthwhile to take inventory.

1. What currencies do you have?

2. How much currency do you have?

3. Which currencies do you need to develop?

Grow your influence and your ability to negotiate with confidence by growing the kinds and amounts of currency you have to offer.

WHAT DO YOU WANT?

Negotiating skills are not just for the workplace. They will serve you in every area of your life.

Do you want your family to pitch in more at home? Do you want to go back to school but your spouse wants you home with the children? Do you want to play a more significant volunteer role? Do you dream of helping abused children, battered women, or the homeless?

These situations are all negotiations. They ask you to define what you want, what you need to make it happen, who can help you reach the goal, and how you will negotiate for a win-win.

If we look at the life of Jesus, we will see that He was a master at integrative bargaining. When people approached Jesus, many times He would ask them, "What do you want Me to do for you?" His sole purpose was to draw people to the Father, yet He saw ways to give them what they needed in exchange for what He wanted—their hearts. As our prime example, His goal was always to reach a win-win.

The story of Ruth and Boaz also contains very direct lessons about negotiation. In the wake of great loss,

Naomi and Ruth negotiated for a new opportunity and a secure future. This is certainly a story of redemption; it is also a tale of negotiation. (There is even a complex land deal thrown in the mix.) These women were brilliant. They created a win for generations to come.

As women of God, we do not need to shy away from what we feel is a cold business tactic. We can incorporate the skills of integrative negotiation to bring value to all those around us. If you want to be more active in ministry, leave the workplace to care for children, reenter the workplace after caring for children, receive higher pay at your current place of employment, or start a small group program at your church, whatever it is, good negotiating skills can take you from where you are to where you want to be.

> As the man came near, Jesus asked him, "What do you want me to do for you?" "Lord," he said, "I want to see!" And Jesus said, "All right, receive your sight! Your faith has healed you." Instantly the man could see, and he followed Jesus, praising God. And all who saw it praised God, too.
>
> —Luke 18:40–43, nlt

CHAPTER 5

Be Clear in Thought and Deed

*A double minded [woman] is
unstable in all [her] ways.*

—JAMES 1:8, KJV

IT'S VERY EASY to become task driven. Unless we are guided by a vision and grounded by a plan, we can become reactive and shortsighted. When that happens, we end up looking more like short-order cooks, checking off the tasks and shouting, "Order up!" Even more discouraging is the real possibility of completing the tasks and falling short of the goal.

What would change about the way you manage your responsibilities if you thought of them as projects instead of tasks? How would your approach change if you started thinking more like a project manager?

Read this chapter with all of your responsibilities—home, work, and ministry—in mind. Look for ways to apply the following disciplines to what is already on your plate:

- Ask defining questions to create a clear picture of expected results.

- Speak more strategically, so people see you as a strategic thinker.

- Make confident decisions based on success criteria.

- Plan more effectively, so important pieces don't fall through the cracks.

- Monitor progress on the way to your goals.

- Keep people informed with relevant information.

- Manage expectations to avoid disappointment with results.

- Turn your stakeholders into shareholders.

- Anticipate and manage risk strategically.

- Imagine the ripple effect of your actions and your nonactions.

These behaviors are the hallmark of effectiveness. As you apply the attributes of project management to your daily tasks, you are more compelling, confident, and prepared.

Project managers are fascinating. The good ones have an eclectic—almost paradoxical—set of skills. They must be tactical and strategic, task oriented and people oriented, marketers, planners, team builders, and communicators. We can learn a great deal from the disciplines of project management and apply these practices to our various responsibilities. We can even use project management success factors to measure effectiveness.

Project success has long been defined as on time, on budget, with high quality. Eric Verzuh in *The Fast Forward MBA in Project Management* gives us another perspective with five factors of success.[1] When you achieve these with your assignments, you have been successful.

1. Agreement on goals

2. A visible, measurable plan with clear accountabilities

3. Effective communication between everyone involved

4. A controlled scope—complete agreement on what the project includes and what it doesn't

5. Endorsement and support

Knowing what makes a project successful is one thing. Knowing how to make that happen is another. The following strategies are about the how, beginning with how assignments are received.

"If you don't know what you're doing, pray to the Father. He loves to help. You'll get his help, and won't be condescended to when you ask for it" (James 1:5).

BE CLEAR ABOUT WHAT IS ASKED OF YOU

Has this ever happened to you?

You are innocently walking down the hallway or working intently. Out of nowhere your boss appears. She has just come from a meeting of some kind or another, and when she sees you, her eyes light up. You've seen that look before,

> but it's too late to run. You are about to receive
> an assignment. This is a drive-by delegation.
>
> While your boss is standing in front of you,
> the assignment makes perfect sense. You get it.
> The moment she moves away, you realize you do
> not have a clue what she wants you to do!

Here's where we can take a page from project management and a lesson from good project managers. It's called project definition, and it keeps you from flailing around in the dark. Here's how project definition works.[2]

The next time someone asks you to do something, make a list of what you know, or think you know, about what they need you to do. Write down every detail you can think of. Then review each item and make another list of questions you have. Follow up with the person who is delegating the task to you to review the specifics and clarify your questions. This is something you can do with the tasks you initiate for yourself as well.

Here are some answers you want to achieve through project definition:

- *What is the goal of this assignment?* What are we trying to accomplish? What is the picture of success? What does the end result look like? Make sure you and those requesting your help have the same crystal-clear vision of the end result.

There is nothing more disappointing than completing an assignment only to find out it isn't what they were looking for.

- *Why is this project important?* How does this assignment impact the priorities of the person or organization? Knowing this adds interest and inspiration to the work and allows you to work in context.

- *Where does this work connect with other work that is going on throughout the organization?* How does my project impact other initiatives, and how do they impact mine? If you don't understand these connections, you may duplicate work or create something others won't or can't use.

- *Who needs to be informed and updated?* Who are the stakeholders? How often would you like to receive updates? Whom will this assignment impact? Understanding whom your work impacts gives you important clues about how you will need to communicate.

- *When does the assignment need to be complete?* What are the significant milestones? Agreement up front on deadlines allows you to control your assignments and makes it less necessary for your boss to micromanage you.

If you set about *doing* before *defining*, your project will be more difficult, less supported, and ultimately less successful. Resist—with all of your might—the temptation to jump into action before you have carefully defined the assignment.

UNDERSTAND WHAT DRIVES YOUR PROJECT

In every project there are drivers. Drivers limit or constrain projects, and project managers use them as decision-making guides. There are three drivers. All three may be important to your assignment, but only one of them is primary:

1. When time is the primary driver, there is an urgency to complete the project. Deadlines are driving you.

2. If money is primary, resources are limited. You must find ways to complete the assignment with a careful eye on costs.

3. Quality speaks to the elegance of a
   project. If quality comes first, you are
   less concerned with how long it takes or
   what it costs. You are more interested in
   adding value (i.e., adding functionality,
   making it easier to use, more unique, or
   harder for a competitor to duplicate).

A Broadway set designer put all of this into perspective for me with one simple question. When commissioned for a new theater set, he responds, "Do you want it fast, cheap, or beautiful? Pick two." This really works!

Think about it. If you want it fast and cheap, it won't be pretty! If you want it cheap and beautiful, it will take longer. And finally, if you want it beautiful and fast, it's going to be expensive.

Knowing what drives your project is important because it gives you a measurement for success, guides your decisions along the way, and helps you manage expectations. When you find yourself at a crossroads—choosing options or solving problems within the project—the driver will point you in the right direction.

- If time is pressing on your assignment,
  you will understand that meeting the
  deadline is more important than making
  it prettier or perfect. You may have a
  thousand creative ideas for making it

better. You could get lost in the possibilities of this project, and if you do, you will miss the mark.

- If money is the issue, you must look for ways to reduce costs and maximize resources. Using our set design as an example, this would mean understanding and focusing on basic requirements.

- If quality is the key success indicator, you are being measured on how special or effective the result is. Manage quality indicators carefully. Make sure everyone agrees in advance how quality will be measured.

I learned to see drivers more clearly through a lens of disappointment. On my own time, I developed a sales curriculum for the organization I worked for at the time. I spent weeks developing a gorgeous training manual. This thing was amazing!

When I proudly presented it to my boss, he flipped through it dismissively and said, "I am more interested in results than graphics. What will it cost to produce this for every sales representative?"

I was devastated. What a bad, bad boss.

In retrospect, I made a couple of big mistakes with that self-initiated project. I failed to understand what was most important to my boss—how he would measure success, what he considered quality.

I presented a training manual to him—a very, very beautiful training manual. But he wasn't interested in a manual. He wasn't in the market for an amazing layout with full-color graphics. He would have been very interested in the results achieved through the training, and that's what I needed to sell. When I didn't sell that quality, he evaluated my project on cost.

Be prepared. If you ask the person you are serving (even if it's yourself) what is most important—time, money, or quality—you are likely to hear, "All of the above." You'll probably need to dig down with some test questions to find out what is really driving your project. Ask questions like:

- If we found a way to make this really amazing, and it meant spending more money, would you want us to do that?

- If we had more time, we could make this even better. Can we have more time?

- We could save money if we eliminate this piece. Would you like to do that?

Once you've isolated the driver, realize it can move on without your permission and without warning. What began as a quality-driven project can quickly become a schedule-driven project, and so on. You are wise to keep your finger on the pulse of your project and the people it will affect to detect even a subtle shift in what drives it.

TURN YOUR STAKEHOLDERS INTO SHAREHOLDERS

Stakeholders are the people who will be affected by your project. They may be the people using the process or report you create or the ones attending an event you coordinate. Your stakeholders may be internal or external customers who will use the product you design or the service you provide. Stakeholders generally have something to gain or lose as a result of your work.

Shareholders, on the other hand, are people who are vested in the project. Yes, like stakeholders, the results of the project will impact them too. But shareholders have a sense of ownership, and ownership is created through involvement. The most successful project managers understand this dynamic, and they work very hard to involve the shareholders throughout the process of the project.

Once you have identified the stakeholders, identify ways to involve and vest them. Here are a few examples:

- Sharon was asked to develop a new employee orientation. She interviewed employees who had been with the company for less than one year to find out what would have made their introduction to the company more helpful. She also asked the corporate training team to advise her on developing a professional presentation. The finished project was welcomed by the employees, and the training team happily incorporated the changes into the corporate orientation process, knowing they had been included and allowed input throughout the project.

- Karen's assignment was to pilot a mentoring program for her company. She created an advisory board—a group of potential mentors and protégés to define the program requirements. This group met several times to create the strategy and develop a presentation to sell the concept. The credibility of the people Karen involved and the quality of their work were so impressive, senior management fully endorsed and funded the program.

- Pam was charged with developing corporate standards and best practices for hiring. She consulted with hiring managers throughout the organization to gain their perspective. When the procedures were drafted, she returned to the hiring managers and invited their feedback. When the procedures were rolled out, the changes were quickly embraced by the hiring managers.

In each of these cases, the stakeholders became part owners in the project. Instead of feeling like something was being done to them, they were treated as customers of the project and resources to it. The women in charge of these projects found ways to leverage internal strengths and create positive visibility for the people who would ultimately own the result.

Especially when your assignment introduces change, involvement will help you reduce resistance and increase cooperation. Some of the best advice I ever received is: "People act best on their own ideas." Or to put it another way: "People don't argue with their own data."

Break It Down, Make It Visible, and Keep Them Informed

Project managers know how to handle their own data. They are experts at breaking even their most complex project into tasks, actions, and deliverables. With outcomes firmly in mind, they identify the steps it will take to get there.

Think of your assignments like jigsaw puzzles, and the tasks inside are the pieces. We set up the puzzle by spreading the pieces out on the table and turning them face up so we can look at them and figure out where they go.

The pieces must fit together to create the picture on the box. Some pieces go in first to create the framework, and we constantly refer to the picture on the box for clues about where pieces go. Missing pieces ruin the picture.

Managing the tasks of your assignment is like putting together a puzzle. The end result, or project goal, is the picture on the box. You have to keep that picture in front of you at all times—never losing sight of the desired outcome.

Begin by brainstorming all the tasks or pieces, and spread them out where you can see them. Project managers use sophisticated tools to break the project down. Or you can keep it simple by putting each task on a separate Post-it note or index card. Brainstorm everything that must be done to achieve the goal. For each task:

- Determine the time requirement.

- Decide how you will measure the success of this piece.

- Identify the risks and opportunities associated with this task: What could go right? What could go wrong? How will we know? When will we know?

- Determine who is responsible for completing this piece.

- Where does the piece fit into the puzzle?

You can answer that question by taking up another aspect of the project manager. They use a bevy of reports, graphs, and flowcharts to make a project's plan visible. They create confidence and build in accountability by ensuring everyone involved knows who is responsible for what.

When people understand what you are working on and the results you are driving toward, you invite confidence, respect, and support. When your plan is visible, you reduce miscommunications, misunderstandings, and missed expectations. It is also easier to imagine the ripple effect of your actions.

Look for ways to make your plans more accessible, more visible, and more meaningful to others. Use calendars, priority lists, and task updates to tell your story, keep everyone informed, and sell your plan.

Project managers carefully construct a communication plan. They use it to create focus, manage expectations, generate interest, maintain support, and market achievements. To be successful, your communication should consider:

- Who needs to know about what you are working on?

- What information is relevant and important to them?

- What is the right format or channel of communication?

- How often do people need to be updated?

In the context of your work, how well are you keeping your shareholders informed? Are you choosing the most effective channels of communication (i.e., formal, informal, in person, in writing, over the phone, and electronic)?

Many people feel overwhelmed with the amount of information they receive on a daily basis. How can you help your shareholders get to the information they need more efficiently?

You may want to ask for some feedback from your

shareholders. Find out if they are getting the information they need from you or if they are receiving information that isn't useful. This will help you monitor your project from the shareholders' point of view.

MONITOR YOUR PROGRESS

At any given moment, project managers know exactly where the project is. They can tell you what is done, what isn't, and what must happen next to keep the project on track.

You can monitor your own progress the same way by understanding where you are at all times in relationship to your goals—by understanding what is on track, what isn't, and what needs to happen right now. When you have that kind of awareness, you build tremendous credibility, and you manage the most important project of all—the project called *you*.

A good example of monitoring your own progress, if you are a career woman, is your performance review. You probably have this discussion at least once a year. Reviews typically include results you have achieved and areas for development and improvement. After you and your manager sign and date the review form, you should receive a copy. What do you do with that copy?

Many employees tell me they put it in a neat little file with other performance reviews and report cards they've collected through the years.

On a monthly or quarterly basis, bring your latest review to a meeting with your boss. Make it a document for discussion. Provide an update. Talk about how you are using the feedback, what you are learning, and the progress you've made. Talk about areas of concern, where you aren't making the progress you'd like to see, and ask for a recommendation.

When you do this, you are honoring and managing the feedback. You are building credibility and demonstrating the ability to manage yourself. You are also setting the stage for your next performance review by managing your boss's perceptions.

ANTICIPATE AND
CALCULATE THE RISKS

In every project there is risk, and project managers are very strategic in how they manage it. You can plan for some risks, and others will surprise you—once. Identify risks to your goals by thinking about what could go wrong.

What could keep you from achieving your objectives? Find the risks hiding inside your work, and decide in advance how you will handle them if they do occur.

There are five things you can do with a risk:[3]

1. Accept risks that are unlikely or will have little impact on your goal. It

probably won't happen, and even if it does, it won't make a huge difference.

2. Avoid significant risks by changing the scope. If the risk is significant and you can step completely around it by altering your plan, you may want to consider doing that.

3. Monitor your work and build in red flags that will alert you if something isn't happening on time or as planned. Have contingency plans in your pocket. When Plan A isn't working, shift decisively to Plan B.

4. Transfer or share the risk by building in guarantees, reimbursements, or fixed prices.

5. Mitigate the risk by working very hard to reduce its likelihood and the impact it will have on what you are trying to accomplish.

All of these decisions about risk have some things in common. It is assumed that you see risks that put your goals in peril, you understand these risks, and you know in advance how you will respond to them.

Put the Finishing Touches On

Closing a project is important, and good project managers know how to put the finishing touches on.

They understand that if you fail to close properly, you miss marvelous opportunities to market results, celebrate achievements, collect lessons learned, and recognize others.

The following are some of the devices project managers use to close the loop, with recommendations for how you might apply them to the work you do.

Project Managers...	You Can...
Conduct a post-project review to compare actual results with the stated goals.	Schedule a meeting to review your goals and results. This is a marvelous way to market your efforts and achievements. It is also good for locating missed expectations and perception gaps.
Present results to project "shareholders" with a project summary report. Then follow up with the people on whom the project had an impact.	Look for opportunities to follow up with the people on whom your work has an impact. Keep them up to date, in the loop, and informed.

Project Managers...	You Can...
Secure client acceptance by asking clients to sign off or approve deliverables and confirm acceptance.	Ask for feedback from your internal and external "customers." Find out how satisfied they are with your work. Ensure their expectations are being met.
Lead postmortems to collect and document lessons learned.	Frequently ask, "What is going well? Why? What isn't? Why? What can we do differently to improve results?" When conducting a postmortem with others, it is important to hold the blame. This dialogue is to reinforce what works and learn from what doesn't. If it becomes an exercise in blaming, defending, or explaining, it won't bring real value. Begin postmortem meetings with clear ground rules to protect the purpose.

Project Managers...	You Can...
Reward and recognize people who contributed to success. Make projects rewarding experiences.	Send thank-you notes and brag about others. Look for ways to recognize, appreciate, and market the people who help you make it happen.
Hand off maintenance and detail unresolved issues with a project turnover memo to stakeholders.	Make quality handoffs so the balls don't drop as they leave your hands. Communicate outstanding issues and ensure those pieces don't fall through the cracks.

LOOK STRATEGIC, SOUND STRATEGIC... EVERY DAY!

Thinking strategically is something women aren't generally known for. I know that's not necessarily fair, but it's true. If you want to create a reputation for being strategic, you must speak in strategic terms. In the guide *FYI: For Your Improvement*, authors Michael Lombardo and Robert Eichinger advise, "Every discipline has its lexicon. In order to be a member, you have to speak the code."[4]

Learn to speak strategically by becoming a student of strategy. Check out best-selling business books, pick up a copy of the *Harvard Business Review*, and study the strategies of successful business leaders. Learning this language is like learning any other language—immersing yourself in it is the best way to speak it fluently. You will find the language of strategy morphs. New words are created to describe emerging strategies or to put a fresh face on old ones.

First we had outsourcing, then offshoring, and now rightshoring. We had paradigms—and then shifts for those. We've used terms like benchmarking, *best practices*, and *organic growth*. I've heard organizations refer to walletshare, mindshare, and heartshare. There are value propositions and value migration, and by the time you read this, the language will have morphed again.

When we apply these disciplines, our work is suddenly more than a giant inbox of tasks and to-dos. There is a strategy to the way we define, plan, manage, and, yes, even the way we communicate. We are more effective and more credible. We enjoy more recognition and support. Others have a greater sense of the value we create—and we have a greater sense of it, too.

Think like a project manager, and remember, the most important project you manage is *you*.

CHAPTER 6

Let Love Reignite Your World

Mostly what God does is love you. Keep company with him and learn a life of love. Observe how Christ loved us. His love was not cautious but extravagant. He didn't love in order to get something from us but to give everything of himself to us. Love like that.

—EPHESIANS 5:2

REMEMBER THE DAY you applied for the job you have now? Remember practicing for your interview and planning what to wear? Remember how nervous you were? Remember thinking and praying, "Pick me! Please pick me!"

And they did. They picked you! Months or even years later, are you still thinking, "I'm so glad they picked me"?

Maybe you're a mom with teenage children and you didn't apply, but you remember the day you were drafted. How excited were you once the news of new life settled in your heart? Are you still excited?

Or you're an empty-nester, remembering the day your husband proposed to you. Do you still enjoy serving him dinner?

Sometimes we need to fall in love with our various roles in life—to remember what we love about them and why we do what we do. One of the best ways to do that is to remember the day they picked (or drafted) you and look for ways to add value to every task, every assignment, every communication, and every relationship. As you read this chapter, I hope you will search for and discover how you can become more valuable, because opportunity always follows value.

The way to secure an abundant future is to become more valuable—more vital. Now for the really good news: you get to decide how valuable and vital you want to be.

INCREASE YOUR VALUE TO CREATE YOUR OPPORTUNITY

You are an asset. You have real value. When you increase your value, you create opportunity. (This has to work. It's the law of sowing and reaping, and it will work for you.)

I encourage you to begin today, right where you are, with the responsibilities you have, to find a way to increase your value. Do that tomorrow too. Do it every day for a week. You were not designed to be a commodity. Your opportunity is calling!

You begin to pull away from the crowd when you look for ways to *add value*. This is where you push beyond base expectations. You add creativity and commitment to your skills to put a little topspin on the ball.

If your boss asks you to gather data for an important presentation, you add value by getting the information you were asked for and considering what else your boss may need to be more fully prepared. Who will be in this meeting? What questions or concerns might they have? You bring the data...and more.

Adding value is the way you appear, prepare, and organize. It can be found in your presentation, your execution, and your follow-through. It is demonstrated in how you understand the needs and exceed the expectations of those you serve.

IDENTIFYING YOUR
SPHERE OF SERVICE

To add real value you may need to rethink who is in your sphere of service and how you can boost your customer service skills. It's easy for us to be nice to, think highly of, and serve well people who are not close to us.

Your "customers" may be external—the neighbor down the street, the vendor at company X, or the events coordinator for a conference you are leading. But you also have internal customers—the people who report to you, your boss, coworkers, friends, or ministry partners. What would change if you began to see and treat all of these people like your most valuable customers? What would change about the way you work if you found the answers to these questions?

- Who are my customers?

- What do my customers need?

- How can I become a greater resource to them?

- How can I make my customers more successful?

- How can I be more responsive?

- How can I anticipate their needs and be more proactive in addressing them?

You create extreme loyalty, credibility, and influence with the people you serve when you demonstrate a solid understanding of their challenges, needs, and expectations. The perception people have of your service is entirely based on that awareness.

If you meet expectations, your service is perceived as satisfactory. If you don't, the service was disappointing. Your service is considered exceptional only when you consistently exceed the people's expectations—when you add value.

"Love and truth form a good leader;
sound leadership is founded on
loving integrity" (Proverbs 20:28).

MAKE IT EASIER FOR PEOPLE TO WORK WITH YOU

At the *user-friendly* level, you make it easier for people to work with you. You are building a strong network and becoming a greater resource to more people.

We've all encountered people who are not easy to work with. They may be very knowledgeable, but they also are resistant and grumpy, unavailable and unapproachable. At some point we look for ways to work around them, and that's when they become less essential to the mission. Less essential is just another way of saying less valuable.

> Lisa is a human resources representative, charged with managing the annual employee benefits enrollment. Each year she sends out hundreds

of employee selection packages. To confirm the packages have been received and the selection deadline is clear, employees are asked to sign and return a confirmation receipt.

In years past, less than 20 percent of the employees confirmed receipt with the initial request. Lisa would spend hours following up with reminders and multiple requests—harping on employees to sign and return the form. Then she asked herself the user-friendly question: "How can I make this step easier for my customers?"

She did a little customer research and tested a few options. Ultimately she decided on an electronic receipt. One week after the benefits packages were distributed, Lisa sent an e-mail to every employee in the organization. In this message, her customers were reminded to look for the package and make a note of the selection deadline. They were also given contact information for questions or to locate a missing package. When the message was opened, an automatic e-mail receipt was generated for Lisa's tracking purposes.

Her solution was successful.

Instead of trying to increase compliance with her process, Lisa viewed the process from her customers' perspective and found a way to make it more user-friendly. When she stopped policing her process, she found a way to improve it.

BRING SOLUTIONS TO THE TABLE

Next, you become more valuable when you search for and deliver *solutions*. At this level you are not waiting to be told what to do. You are actively engaged in the process of continuous improvement. Here you are looking for:

- What costs too much?

- What takes too long?

- What is poor in quality?

- What falls through the cracks?

- What is outdated, inefficient, or ineffective?

- Where are we missing an opportunity?

Some problems you can solve on your own. When you do, find a way to market your results in quantifiable terms. When you save the company time or money, find a way to tell that story!

Sometimes you can't solve the problem on your own. In those cases you'll need to sell your solutions to others. That means doing your homework and presenting your ideas in a compelling way. Here your goal is to influence the people who can give your ideas legs to run on.

Search for Best Practices

My work in talent management and mentoring programs exposes me to many industries and fields. I find common challenges and meet the most innovative people. Together we search for effective ways to identify and develop leadership. We look for best practices. What I learn from my experience with one organization can be of tremendous value for another.

Over time we have created a community, a network of professionals who share what they are learning. We have built a bank of best practices. The bank is a way for people to deposit and withdraw ideas, showcase their successes, and openly discuss their challenges. The currency is innovation, and I have the distinct pleasure of being a best-practices broker.

You can broker best practices too. Help those you serve anticipate the future by stepping out of your zone to compare processes and search for best practices in other areas. Build a broad network of contacts, and make it a goal to learn from them:

- What do they see on the horizon?

- What are they doing to prepare for it?

- Even though you serve in different fields, what common challenges do you face?

- What processes do you have in common?

- How are they addressing the challenges?

This is a wonderful way to network. People enjoy talking about what they are learning and producing. And you may have the answer they have been searching for. When that happens, you become a contributor in their success.

FIND YOURSELF AND
STRETCH YOURSELF

If you are feeling like a commodity at work or at home, this isn't a message telling you to fall on your sword or pack up your toys and go home. It is your call to action. I don't think this process is necessarily linear. You may find ways to add value and create solutions simultaneously.

While it's not linear, I believe it would be very difficult to move from the commodity level to anticipating the future overnight. You build credibility, influence, and a deep understanding of those in your sphere of service at levels below that. Once that foundation is firmly in place, you will have the currency you need to make a real impact on the future.

Resolve to begin where you are and look for ways to operate more fully at other levels of value. The very moment you decide to increase your value, the process has already begun.

The truth of this model was a painful, eye-opening reality for Carolyn. I met her at a conference, and I'll never forget her. She could not hold back tears as she told her story.

About a year before, Carolyn had accepted a new job. In the beginning she was so excited with the opportunity. She couldn't work hard enough, stay late enough, come in early enough, or volunteer enough.

Some of her expectations of the job weren't met. At first she was able to overlook these disappointments. But as time went on, resentment crept in. She stopped coming in early and working late. She quit volunteering for special projects.

She withdrew her value.

She finished her story with these words: "I'm at this conference to save my job. I am now considered a performance problem, and this workshop is part of my performance improvement plan."

Sometimes opportunity doesn't arrive as quickly as you'd like. It may not even come to you where you work now. But when you add value, opportunity absolutely, positively will show up. It's a rule! What you sow, you will reap.

Are you disappointed with where you are in life? Have you been making value withdrawals? Stop it!

By the way, when it matters the most, you won't feel

like practicing anything you've learned here. That's why they call it discipline, and that's why doing it sets you apart—the average person won't.

Something else happens when you apply this model. You will enjoy your life and the people you serve, your work, and your ministry! You will feel more empowered, engaged, and motivated. You don't rely on other people to pull commitment out of you. Your commitment comes from a place inside of yourself.

Being valuable is energizing and challenging. As you consistently add value, you instantly revamp the purpose for why you do what you do. Your confidence will come from the value you bring and the difference you make.

INVEST IN THE
SUCCESS OF OTHERS

Another way to bring back the love for what you do is to lead others to the next level of performance or assist them in achieving their goals. They grow, we grow, and we create an amazing legacy. There are so few women coaches or mentors, but the value it brings to us in immeasurable.

Coaching focuses on the current position, improving performance by developing a person's knowledge and skills. Mentoring reaches into the future by developing the skills, knowledge, understanding, and connections that release potential and unlock possibility. Clearly, both are important, and occasionally they run in parallel. Even so, it's important to recognize the difference between the two and honor the purpose of each.

Regardless of whether you directly manage people or not, you have the opportunity—the obligation even—to coach and mentor others. I think you'll find it's in your own best interest to be a great coach, and mentoring is one of the most rewarding things you will ever do.

> Debra had been struggling for several months in her sales role. Normally a top producer, consistently exceeding every target, she found herself in a dry place. For ninety-nine different reasons—most of which she doesn't personally control—her production dropped considerably. Her confidence fell with it.
>
> Seeing how this difficult sales environment was impacting her, Debra's boss asked if she would be willing to coach several new employees as they came up to speed on the product line. Debra was happy to do it.
>
> As she looks back on those frustrating months, the coaching assignment is the bright spot. "I was so discouraged with my production," she recalls. "When my boss asked me to be a coach, it was a vote of confidence at just the right the time. I was able to help the new sales associates come up to speed quickly. I made a real difference for those people. As I coached them, my

confidence was restored. I know now that was the whole plan, and I'm grateful for a boss with that kind of insight." Bravo, boss!

LEAVE PEOPLE BETTER
THAN YOU FOUND THEM

One of the loveliest people I know is retiring. Her name is Frances, and she leaves behind a rich legacy. As she steps into the next season of her life, her work lives on in those she has developed, mentored, and encouraged along the way. She is so admired and respected, there isn't even the notion of replacing her. We know that cannot be done.

Surely the work will get done, but Frances can never be replaced.

Over the years, Frances became a resource for people within her organization, her field, and her community. Some of these people worked for her, and some worked with her. She reported to a few of them, and many of the people who benefited from her knowledge and experience now work for other organizations.

Frances was often asked for her advice and counsel because she is wise and trustworthy. People knew they could trust her with their ideas and challenges, even their humanness. She didn't bang people over the head with advice. Instead she helped people sort through the issues to discover options.

There are dozens of things that make Frances irreplaceable. But if there was only one thing I could point to—one attribute that defined her most—it would be this: she leaves everyone better than she found them.

That is my goal too. My personal mission is to leave people a little better than I found them—a little more encouraged and optimistic about the future. A little more skilled. Feeling a little more valued, confident, and prepared for what is to come.

What I have learned from Frances, consulting with her on various projects through the years, is a gentle balance between the concern for people and the concern for results. She never sacrificed people for results, or results for people. She searched for ways to bring the best out in people, to achieve results. She invested herself fully in every project—especially the people projects. And she never lost sight of her core purpose and passion.

Frances invested in me too. Many of my clients are referrals from her extensive network. I am the grateful beneficiary of her credibility and influence.

That is how Frances invested in others and built a bridge to the future. I smile when I think of the people who will cross that bridge—stepping surely into a new place with new possibilities.

The Call to Strength

Using a dull ax requires great strength,
so sharpen the blade. That's the value
of wisdom; it helps you succeed.

—ECCLESIASTES 10:10, NLT

I HAVE ALWAYS BEEN a collector of ideas, tools, and tactics—reading ferociously—being inspired and challenged by new approaches and the best ways to do everyday things. Before I could afford to, I began building a library of resources.

My favorite retreat is still the bookstore. Some of my best mentors have met with me in the pages of a book. Unlike some of my favorite women, I think one *can* have too many shoes, but it would be very difficult to have too many books or too many ideas. Over the years, the collection of titles and authors has grown considerably, and I have learned that collecting ideas isn't enough. You must use them.

Sometimes as I look over an audience, I make a confession: "What I have to say isn't all new. It's likely, even probable, that you will hear some things you've heard before, presented in a new way, or with new application." Sometimes the best ideas are timeless and the most profound concepts are surprisingly simple.

The point isn't: Do you know this stuff? The point is: Are you really doing it? Are you applying what you know and practicing what you have learned?

The same is true with potential. Potential is worthless until it is released and realized. I've met plenty of people with extraordinary potential who will never amount to anything of real value. They lack discipline, resiliency, and consistency. They give up too easily and aren't willing to pay the price. It's frustrating to work with people like that because, at some point, you realize you want something for them more than they want it for themselves.

Anything worthwhile will always cost you something. It will stretch you. If it doesn't, it's not a goal— it's just another nice idea in your collection.

In the end it really isn't about what you know. It's about what you do. By now I hope you've isolated what you will do to put these ideas to work. These choices and steps are very personal, and they accumulate— they become who you are and what you are known for.

SPEAK IT

I am a big believer in affirmations—speaking what is powerful and positive into my life and the lives of others. I believe the ancient power of the blessing is available to us even now. "The LORD will send a *blessing* on your barns and on everything you put your hand to. The LORD your God will bless you in the land he is giving you" (Deuteronomy 28:8, NIV, emphasis added).

I encourage you to turn your goals into positive affirmations and read them aloud every day. Speak them as if they were already true. The following are affirmations you can use to speak the concepts we discussed in this book into your life.

- I am designed for success. I have unique strengths and abilities, and my opportunities are waiting for me.

- I soften my inner dialogue and manage my personal messages from the inside out. I have an important story to tell, and I tell it well.

- I empower myself with options, role clarity, accountability, and optimism.

- I am a positive catalyst. I bring solutions.

- I equip myself with emotional awareness.

- I walk in a spirit of gratitude.

- I have the confidence to negotiate. I know what I want, I believe I deserve it, and I feel powerful enough to ask for it.

- I lead from my current position by raising the standard and demonstrating extreme initiative.

- I am effective even when the people around me are not.

- I am strategic.

- I secure my future by serving from a place of love. My service to others is valuable and vital. I am building a bridge to my future.

- I turn my stakeholders into shareholders.

- I invest in the success of others.

- I break through the barriers to establish productive relationships. I turn my adversaries into allies and invite a spirit of collaboration.

- I add value to everything I do. I am creative. I am a valuable resource.

- I am designed for success, and I am creating a reputation that opens the door of opportunity and unlocks my possibility.

A FINAL BLESSING FOR
THE WOMAN OF GOD

As I have written this book, I have prayed for the women who will read it. I have prayed for you: That you might find the inspiration, encouragement, and tools you need to release your potential and realize your possibility, to be the strong woman of God you were meant to be. That you would discover ideas that help you become more vital and valuable, recognized and rewarded.

This book won't change you or your circumstances. It's what you do with the ideas in this book that will make the difference. In that way, I am honored if I have played even a small part in unfolding your possibility.

I wish you the very best and leave you with this blessing:

> *May God prosper the work of your hands and the work of your heart;*
> *May you be surrounded by people who will encourage your dreams, celebrate your victories, and if you should forget, let God remind you who you are;*

May the obstacles in your path serve only to equip and strengthen you;

May the difference you make and the value you create be remarkable; and

As you design your life, may the blessings of God overtake you.

NOTES

CHAPTER 1
SOFTEN YOUR INNER DIALOGUE

1. Stephanie Chaffins, et al., "The Glass Ceiling: Are Women Where They Should Be?" Education, March 22, 1995, abstract available at http://www.highbeam.com/doc/1G1-17039288.html (accessed June 7, 2011).

2. Stephen R. Covey, *The Seven Habits of Highly Effective People* (New York: Fireside, 1990).

3. Brian Tracy, *Psychology of Achievement* (Niles, IL: Nightingale-Conant, 1998).

4. Lawrence B. Stein and Stanley L. Brodsky, "When Infants Wail: Frustration and Gender as Variables in Distress Disclosure," *Journal of General Psychology* 122, no. 1 (1995): 19–27.

5. Bert Decker, *High Impact Communication* (Niles, IL: Nightingale-Conant, 1992).

CHAPTER 2
EMPOWER AND EQUIP YOURSELF

1. Roger Connors, Tom Smith, and Craig Hickman, *The Oz Principle: Getting Results Through Individual and Organizational Accountability* (New Jersey: Prentice Hall Press, 1994).

2. John G. Miller, *Flipping the Switch: Unleash the Power of Personal Accountability Using the QBQ!* (New York: Penguin Group, 2006), 10.

3. Jeff Davidson, "Optimism in an Era of Uncertainty," *Public Management*, November 2004.

4. Jim Collins, *Good to Great: Why Some Companies Make the Leap...and Others Don't* (New York: HarperBusiness, 2001), 199.

5. Martin E. P. Seligman, *Learned Optimism: How to Change Your Mind and Your Life* (New York: Pocket Books, 1990, 1998).

6. Jack Canfield, Mark Victor Hansen, and Les Hewitt, *The Power of Focus: How to Hit Your Business, Personal and Financial Targets With Absolute Certainty* (Deerfield Beach, FL: HCI, 2000).

7. Covey, *The Seven Habits of Highly Effective People*.

CHAPTER 3
GROW YOUR EMOTIONAL INTELLIGENCE

1. Adele B. Lynn, *The EQ Difference: A Powerful Plan for Putting Emotional Intelligence to Work* (New York: AMACOM, a division of American Management Association, 2005).

2. Adapted from Consortium for Research on Emotional Intelligence in Organizations, "Emotional Competence Framework: Personal Competence," http://www.eiconsortium.org/research/emotional_competence_framework.htm (accessed August 29, 2007).

3. Thomas Stirr, *Miller's Bolt: A Modern Business Parable* (New York: Basic Books, 1997).

4. Covey, *The Seven Habits of Highly Effective People*, 242.

CHAPTER 4
ASK FOR WHAT YOU WANT

1. Linda Babcock and Sara Laschever, *Women Don't Ask: Negotiation and the Gender Divide* (Princeton, NJ: Princeton University Press, 2003).

2. Roger Fisher, William Ury, and Bruce Patton, *Getting to Yes: Negotiating Agreement Without Giving In*, 2nd ed. (New York: Penguin Books, 1991).

3. Ibid.

4. Richard E. Walton and Robert B. McKersie, *A Behavioral Theory of Labor Negotiations: An Analysis of a Social Interaction System* (New York: McGraw-Hill, Inc., 1965).

5. Fisher, Ury, and Patton, *Getting to Yes.*

6. Allan R. Cohen and David L. Bradford, *Influence Without Authority* (New York: John Wiley & Sons, Inc., 1989, 1991).

CHAPTER 5
BE CLEAR IN THOUGHT AND DEED

1. Eric Verzuh, *The Fast Forward MBA in Project Management*, 2nd ed. (Hoboken, NJ: John Wiley & Sons, Inc., 2005).

2. Project Management Institute, Inc., *A Guide to the Project Management Body of Knowledge* (Newton Square, PA: Project Management Institute, Inc., 2004).

3. Ibid.

4. Michael M. Lombardo and Robert W. Eichinger, *FYI: For Your Improvement*, 4th ed. (Minneapolis, MN: Lominger Limited, Inc., 2004).

SAY **GOOD-BYE** TO
"**JUST GETTING BY**"
AND **STEP INTO A LIFE**
THAT YOU **LOVE**

978-1-59979-237-8 / $21.99

978-1-59979-466-2 / $21.99

978-1-59979-857-8 / $21.99

Discover how to make the most of your career opportunities and perform your job with passion and excellence.

Learn how to rediscover your passion, overcome your fears, and create the life you've always wanted.

Learn how to plan for success and make yourself indispensable no matter where you work.

You Were Designed for Success and Built to Grow! Get a Move On!

dondi
SCUMACI.inc

You are personally invited to visit www.dondiscumaci.com to get connected, stay energized, and do what you were built for… succeed! Stop by soon to explore these free tools and resources:

- **High-impact ideas to empower and equip you**
- **World-class blog connecting you to a vibrant community**
- **Podcasts for inspiration on the go**
- **Interviews with experts and thought leaders**
- **Events that will help you release your potential and achieve your goals**

Bring Dondi to your organization!

If you would like to bring Dondi to your organization, visit www.dondiscumaci.com for details on booking and availability.